THE JESUIT MARTYRS
OF NORTH AMERICA

The Jesuit Martyrs
of North America

Isaac Jogues, John de Brébeuf, Gabriel Lalemant
Noel Chabanel, Anthony Daniel, Charles Garnier
René Goupil, John Lalande

JOHN J. WYNNE, S. J.

THE UNIVERSAL KNOWLEDGE FOUNDATION
NEW YORK

To the Right Reverend

EDMUND F. GIBBONS, D.D.,

Bishop of Albany;

The diocese in which the Martyrs crimsoned
with their blood the soil of North
America, and which now has the
honor of having opened the roll
of our beloved country's
calendar of the
Blessed.

PREFACE

NEITHER myth nor legend is needed by our country for the heroic story with which every people loves to immortalize its origins. Our earliest history is one of heroes who achieved their wonders, not by physical prowess merely, but by moral grandeur. Their most wonderful achievement is the incomparable devotion with which they, all men of exquisite culture and refinement, labored among human beings who had fallen from man's high estate into the depths of barbarism and depravity. In common with all heroes, they were animated by the noblest passions; but they excelled in love, the greatest of all. They excelled also in the objects of their love, entirely devoid as it was of selfishness, and centred purely on the highest things, on God and on human souls. They are the heroes of the invisible, the spiritual, the supernatural; and these, by word and work, they bring vividly before our weaker vision.

The story of the Martyrs has been repeated so often and by such skilful narrators that it has become a household tale in this country and in Canada. It cannot be told too often. Hitherto it has appeared in books or chapters about one or other of the principals, or as part only of a general history to which it is subordinated. In this book it is for the first time woven together into one complete narrative. In doing this I have availed of the writings of Martin, de Rochemonteix, and Gilmary Shea; of Jones, Campbell, and Devine, with whom I have been closely associated; of Parkman, Bancroft, my friend Dr. John Finley, and especially of the noble publication of the Jesuit Relations by Thwaites and his scholarly editorial staff.

I am indebted to the publishers of "The Jesuit Relations and Allied Documents" for their cordial permission to use their translation of the Relations in the many quotations I have thought well to make from that collection. No one can tell the story of a Brébeuf or of a Jogues better than themselves. I am indebted also to Mr. C. F. Wemyss Brown and Miss Catherine M. Neale for their kindness in assisting me with the revision of both manuscript and proof, and to Frank P. Seaman for his valuable map of the Jesuit Missions in New France.

THE AUTHOR.

June 21, 1925.

CONTENTS

CHAPTER ONE
A Half-Century of Names and Deeds Immortal
A. D. 1600–1650

CHAPTER TWO
Martyrs in Formation
A. D. 1617–1630

CHAPTER THREE
The Missions of New France
A. D. 1608–1614

CHAPTER FOUR
Missionaries—Layman, Friar and Jesuit
A. D. 1615–1625

[ix]

CONTENTS

CHAPTER FIVE

The Missionary's Fortune

A. D. 1626–1628

CHAPTER SIX

Missions and Civilization

A. D. 1632–1634

CHAPTER SEVEN

An Apostle and His Mission

A. D. 1634–1636

CHAPTER EIGHT

CHAPTER NINE

Arrival of Jogues and Garnier

A. D. 1636–1640

CHAPTER TEN

Brébeuf's Ideal Realized

A. D. 1639

[x]

CONTENTS

[xi]

ILLUSTRATIONS

MAPS

THE JESUIT MARTYRS
OF NORTH AMERICA

CHAPTER ONE
A Half-Century of Names and Deeds Immortal
ANNO DOMINI 1600–1650

The first half of the Seventeenth Century—Rulers and Leaders —Genius in literature—Birthtime of modern science—Philosophy, Painting, Sculpture, Music, Education—Schools of the Jesuits— Religion—Great Saints—Influence in civil life—Missionary spirit, Organization—Missions of the Jesuits—A Society baptized in blood—Genius of sanctity imperishable.

DURING the first half of the seventeenth century men were born and things done that were destined to have a lasting influence. Ferdinand II of Germany, in his successful struggle for the Counter-Reformation and the restitution of church properties to their rightful owners, had to sustain the burden of the Thirty Years' War for more than half its duration. Maximilian, Duke and Elector of Bavaria, was ably supporting him, and consolidating in Bavaria the religious spirit for which it is noted to this day. By maintaining peace in France for twenty years, and promoting agricultural, industrial and commercial prosperity, Henry IV prepared the way for Louis XIII, during whose reign, favored as he was with ministers like Colbert and Richelieu, genius was at its best in France. It was the day of such brilliant leaders as Tilly, Wallenstein, Gustavus Adolphus, Turenne, to whom military science and strategy even in our time is much indebted.

[1]

In England, Shakespeare was writing "Hamlet"; rare Ben Jonson, "Every Man in His Humor"; Fletcher, "The Faithful Shepherdess"; Massinger, "A New Way to Pay Old Debts"; blind old Milton, his "Paradise Lost"; Lord Bacon, his "Novum Organum". In Spain, Calderon was creating his "El Principe Constante"; Alarcon, "La Verdad Sospechosa"; Lope de Vega, his "Comedies of the Cloak and Sword"; De Castro, "Las Mocedades del Cid"; and the immortal Cervantes, the immortal "Don Quijote de La Mancha". In France, Corneille was producing "Le Cid"; Molière had begun his stage career; and Richelieu, in 1635, was founding the Academy, which has since been the inspiration of literary work all the world over, as well as in its own country. Among its first members were Boileau, Bossuet, La Fontaine and Racine.

In Italy Baldi was making idyllic poetry and admirable monographs; Davanzati was translating Tacitus; Tassoni parodied the heroic poets in his comic epic; Chiabrera adapted Greek and Latin metres to Italian verse; Testi wrote patriotic poems; and the versatile Salvator Rosa indulged in satire. In Germany, Arndt was writing widely-read books of Protestant theology; the mystic shoemaker Böhme was producing his profound though confused notions; Ayrer and Heinrich, Duke of Brunswick were writing plays; Opitz was bringing forth his masterly treatise on German poetry;

Logau, his epigrams; Fleming, lyrics; Dach's poetry lent lustre to the Königsberg Circle; Gryphius was the chief dramatist of the period; the Jesuit von Spee was intrepidly defending the victims of the witchcraft tribunals; Angelus Silesius was giving noble expression to mysticism in poetry; the Jesuit Balde sang in both German and Latin; von Grimmelshausen, author of the prose classic of the century, "Simplicissimus", was born in 1625.

It was the birthtime of the science we are cultivating to-day, the age of Galileo and his telescope, Torricelli and his barometer, Napier and his logarithms, Huygens' astronomical discoveries, Mersenne and his laws of vibration, Gassendi the Bacon of France, Gilbert and magnets, Harvey and the circulation of the blood, Bacon and the process of induction, Kircher the versatile Jesuit, with his hieroglyphs, adding-machine, speaking-tube and Aeolian harp, Malpighi and his physiology, Roberval the mathematician, Kepler and planets, Gascoigne and his micrometer, Van Helmont and gases, Buonaventura Cavalieri and the geometric method of indivisibles, Sydenham and epidemic diseases, von Guericke and the air-pump.

Spinoza, Descartes, Pascal and Locke were born at the time; their philosophies still influence profoundly the thought and conduct of multitudes. Grotius was gleaning from the neo-Scholastics and mediaeval jurisprudence principles of an interna-

1

tional law which, if honored in our day, would facilitate the establishment of a world's court.

Painters like Velasquez, Murillo, Rembrandt, Rubens, Grimaldi, Lorrain, Reni, Domenichino, Dolci, Sassoferrato, Salvator Rosa, Maratta, Zurbaran were creating their immortal masterpieces. In sculpture, Montanez was enriching the cathedral of Seville; Bernini was at work upon his "Apollo and Daphne"; Maderna was elaborating the death-like pose of his St. Cecilia; Algardi was founding the School of Bologna. In music, the Masters of the Golden Age included Sweelinck, the talented brothers Anerio, da Vittoria, the Englishmen Byrd, Wilbye, Morley, and Gibbons, the Germans Hassler and Aichinger. The first oratorio was produced by Emilio Cavalieri; the first opera, by Peri; Monteverde was the pioneer of modern harmony. Schütz elaborated polyphonic principles in Church music; and Frescobaldi composed for the organ.

Education, particularly in France, was in honor, nowhere more than in the colleges at Clermont, La Flèche and Rouen, which will be frequently mentioned in these pages. So much in favor were the Jesuit colleges in France that from twenty in number before A. D. 1600 they increased to seventy in these fifty years, an average of one a year. In spite of the opposition of the Paris University and the Parliament of Paris, and of false accusations of political enemies, they became the popular schools of the time, their average attendance approximating one thousand. For two centuries they educated men who became leaders in every sphere of life, Corneille, Molière, Descartes, Mersenne, Bossuet, Francis de Sales, Richelieu, Montesquieu, Buffon, Malesherbes. These schools were in close touch with the culture not of France only, but of the learned world of the time. Nationalism had not yet put up barriers to the companionship of scholars of different countries; there was one language in which scholars could converse; travel was leisurely and as often for observation and the exchange of ideas as for trade or pleasure; members of a missionary order were constantly in contact with those who had seen other lands and known other peoples. It is surprising how quickly, without railroad or radio, news got abroad and mental work became common. There was a newspaper in Frankfort in 1615, in Antwerp in 1616, and in England in 1622. Corneille's "Le Cid" appeared in France in 1636; it was produced in England in 1637; that tragedy influenced the European stage for two centuries. Drama was a notable element in the Jesuit system of education, and a point of contact between them and the official and lettered world. It was not unusual for the court and nobility to attend their college plays, and for cities like Munich and Paris to solemnize these productions. Jesuit professors wrote these plays and directed their performance and other similar public exhibitions. One of the few facts recorded of Jogues as professor in the college at Rouen is the reading of a Latin poem on a legend from Evagrius to the student body, numbering nineteen hundred, at the beginning of the scholastic year 1632.

Arts and science were the main courses in these colleges. In many places, as at Bordeaux, Cahors, Bruges, Reims, Caen and Poitiers, they were affiliated to the universities of these cities, in some cases constituting the university Faculty of Arts. Clermont and Pont-à-Mousson had the complete university courses of the period, theology, philosophy, embracing natural philosophy or science, the humanities, languages, history and literature. We are not surprised, therefore, to find men trained in these colleges, who afterward became missionaries, versed in sacred science, familiar as Jogues and Brébeuf with Holy Writ, but making their own observations astronomical and meteorological, charting maps, noting what was peculiar in forestry, vegetation and animal life, recording the racial characteristics of the Indians—one of them, Lafitau, is the founder of modern ethnology[1]—studying their languages not only as missionaries, but as philologists, and planning as true political economists, like Le Jeune, the civilization that flourishes in Canada to-day. The Ontario Government in 1920 published Potier's seven books on the Huron language and grammar.[2]

In those days, at least in countries which had resisted the innovations of Luther, Calvin and Henry VIII, religion was not yet excluded from ordinary life. France had resisted Lutheranism, and Calvinism had not succeeded in winning over many of its people. French Protestants, generally known as Huguenots, were active in trade, and especially in politics, until in 1628 Richelieu put an end to their political pretensions, and to their dealings with her ancient enemy, England, with a view to making Protestantism a dominant factor in the national life. Great saints were common. Like de Sales, Vincent de Paul and Bellarmine, they took prominent part in civil, social and scientific affairs. De Sales wrote books on spiritual subjects which to-day are read for style as much as for content. De Paul organized public charities in a manner and on a scale which no one had before attempted. Bellarmine was the exponent of genuine democracy, especially as we know it in America, and he was the friend who favored consideration for Galileo. Writers like Baronius, Petavius, Bossuet, Lessius, de Paz were bequeathing a heritage in history, positive theology, apologetics, and mysticism which has not yet been exhausted. Paul V had succeeded in making the enactments of the Council of Trent the established discipline of the Church.

So active was the missionary spirit at the time that Gregory XV found it necessary to constitute a permanent congregation for the propagation of the Faith, the Propaganda. Paul had solemnized the beatification of many, like Ignatius Loyola, Francis Xavier, Philip Neri, Teresa, Louis Bertrand, Thomas of Villanova, Isidore, and the canonization of Charles Borromeo, Frances of Rome. Gregory had canonized Ignatius, Francis, Philip, Teresa and Isidore, and beatified among others Albertus Magnus and Peter of Alcantara. It fell to the lot of Urban VIII to issue the bulls for the canonization of Ignatius and Xavier. He canonized Elizabeth of Portugal and Andrew Corsini. Indeed, so common was it to have petitions to beatify and canonize distinguished servants of God, that he found it necessary to regulate the canonical processes for this purpose. It was an era of holiness, and it was an era of missions likewise. Urban was zealous in promoting both. Saints Peter Fourier and Cousin Germaine, Francis Regis and John Berchmans were actually living. The Church in France needed no reforming agency from without. Vincent de Paul, Olier, Condren, Eudes, Bourdoise were re-creating the clergy and the missionary spirit. The Oratorians under Bérulle, the Vincentians and Capuchins were evangelizing rich and poor, lettered and unlettered. De Sales had brought the cloister close to the world with his Visitandines; de Paul had organized his Daughters of Charity, whom we honor to-day as Sisters of Charity; Eudes his Good Shepherd; and the Ursulines had three hundred and twenty houses for the instruction of young girls, sharing with Notre Dame the education of girlhood in France. To the schools of the Jesuits, Condren was looking for recruits to the Duke de Ventadour's Battalion of the Holy Sacrament, the lay auxiliaries of this true Catholic renascence and the generous supporters of every good movement, especially of the Missions Etrangères, which were to develop in 1658 as a result of all this earnestness and devotion.

Never before nor since was exploration so active. To mention only what was happening in our own world, a de Monts was occupying Port Royal in Acadia in 1604. The English were in Virginia in 1607. Hudson was in New York Bay in 1609. The Dutch were on Manhattan in 1614. By 1634 settlements were made in Massachusetts, New Hampshire, Maine, Maryland, Connecticut, Rhode Island, and Delaware.

Missionary orders had their men in every part of the globe. The Jesuits alone were in China, India, Japan, Cochin-China, Mingrelia (Transcaucasia), Ceylon, Aethiopia, Sierra Leone, Congo, Tibet, Paphlagonia, Persia, Armenia, Angola, Abyssinia, Paraguay, Mexico, Peru, Quito, Maryland and Quebec. From every quarter, word was being received of sacrifices as well as of conquests for the Faith. It was enough to warm the blood of any young religious to hear that, in 1614 alone, one

hundred thousand were made Christians in Paraguay, and then to learn that a Claver had died in
his heroism in Cartagena; that, one after another,
a Chimura, Ribera, Spinola, de Angelis, Andrada,
Carvalho had won the martyr's crown; that without leaving Europe a Melchior and Stephen had
been put to death in Poland; that across the
Channel in England a Bennet, Bradley, Turner,
Jenison, Holland, Corbie, Morse, Owen, Oldcorne
and Garnet were being racked, drawn, hanged and
quartered, in a vain attempt to force them to
betray their brethren as well as to deny their Faith.

Truly the Society of Jesus, to which they
belonged, had been baptized in blood. Within
sixty years after its foundation, eighty-one of its
members had died for religion. Before it was
a half-century older, one hundred and seven
more had sealed their testimony with their lives.
Martyrdom was as much a prospect for its members
as any other, and the self-sacrifice that would lead
up to it was part of the training in its schools, as
much as excellence in arts or science. If men born
and things done in those days were destined by
virtue of genius in art or science to endure in fame
or influence, much more were those who excelled in
the genius of sanctity, to phrase the suggestion of
Aubrey De Vere[3], elected by God to do things which
will never fade from memory, and to be immortal
themselves in happiness and influence.

CHAPTER TWO
Martyrs in Formation
A. D. 1617-1630

Jesuit Martyrs of North America—The priests, Jogues, Brébeuf, Daniel, Garnier, Lalemant, Chabanel—Their devoted companions, Goupil and Lalande, laymen—The Society of Jesus, spirit and training—Life in the novitiate—The Spiritual Exercises—Reformation not an ideal, but a means to the following of Christ—The Exercises and the phobias, athletes of Christ—After the novitiate, studies, philosophy, teaching, theology, priesthood.

A MONG the men of the distinguished half-century outlined in the preceding chapter, whose life-work has had a lasting influence, and whose fame, exalted as it has been up to this, has now become sacred and imperishable, are the eight missionaries who are known as the Jesuit Martyrs of North America.

The singular distinction of being the first in this part of the New World to be so honored belongs to Isaac Jogues, John de Brébeuf, Noel Chabanel, Anthony Daniel, Charles Garnier, Gabriel Lalemant, priests, and their companions, René Goupil and John Lalande, laymen. They were all born in France. They left that country when equipped for their life's work to dwell and labor in the vast and unattractive wilderness known as Canada or New France, three of them, Jogues, Goupil and Lalande, penetrating into territory now part of the State of New York and dying there for the Faith.

The sole object of these intrepid missionaries was

the conversion of the savages who occupied these countries, principally the Hurons, Petuns, Neuters, Algonquins and Iroquois. Never did mortal men work so persistently, nor with such optimism amid every form of privation, obstacle, hardship, danger and reason for discouragement. Only for testimony which inspires conviction, what they endured would be incredible. Like giants they stand out even among their own heroic associates. Their savage tormenters ate the hearts and drank the blood of Lalemant and Brébeuf, hoping to partake of their courage and endurance.

With the exception of Brébeuf who was born March 25, 1593, these martyrs were born and died in the first half of the seventeenth century. He was the only one to exceed fifty years of age, dying in 1649. In that brief space they accomplished the work of long years. The preparation for their arduous careers was the same for all. Of the earliest years of some of them little is known prior to their entrance into the Society of Jesus. After that their manner of life is known minutely, in their various habitations and occupations, up to the time when those who were to become priests received Holy Orders. Fortunately, the schools in which they studied and taught, "the best schools in the world," Bancroft says,[4] are still so celebrated that one may, without surmise, appreciate the seriousness of their formation and the quality of the labor they were appointed to perform.

Jogues, the first of these priests to die a martyr, was born in Orleans, January 10, 1607. According to Canon Hubert, genealogist of Orleans, he was the child of his father's second marriage. The father, who had occupied every prominent official position in his native city, died soon after, leaving the boy's education to the mother, Françoise de Saint-Mesmin. His name Isaac was apparently a favorite one in his family, one of his uncles being so named and two nephews also. Canon Hubert records his name as Jacques, or James, but his townsman and biographer, Forest, whom all follow, names him Isaac, from the baptismal record of the Church of St. Hilary, and the name has been consecrated by usage.[5] Holweck lists forty-eight saints of that name, so that it is not a singularity in Jogues' case.[6] The name fitted him perfectly, predestined as he was to sacrifice. Finishing his college course at seventeen, be became a Jesuit novice at Rouen, leaving there in 1625 to study philosophy three years at the royal college of La Flèche, which Descartes, who studied there, considered one of the most celebrated schools in Europe.[7] After three years more given to teaching he prepared for Holy Orders by the study of theology. Ordained early in 1636, he celebrated his first Mass on February 10th, at Orleans, to the great delight of his family. He departed for Canada on April 2nd, in company with the Governor of New France, Charles Huault de

Montmagny, appointed to succeed Champlain who had died the year before.

The first-born of the group, Brébeuf, appears on the scene only at his entrance into the Jesuit novitiate at Rouen, already twenty-four years of age. He was Norman, born at Condé-sur-Vire, near Lisieux, home of the Little Flower, and not far from Bayeux, famous for its tapestry. There had been Crusaders in his family, and two centuries before a Brébeuf had fought with William the Conqueror at Hastings. Thence, no doubt, came English descendants of the family, the Arundels, with their own three illustrious martyrs, Philip Howard, the Duke of Norfolk, his father, and William Howard, Viscount Stafford.[8] This may account for the memorial window in memory of Brébeuf in the Anglican Church of St. Martin at Brighton.[9] He had studied the humanities and philosophy and moral theology also, each for two years, when he entered the Jesuit novitiate in 1617. His health was poor, and he could not make the usual studies of the young Jesuit, nor could he teach for any length of time. Obliged to rest in the Jesuit residence, opened a few years before at Pontoise, he studied theology sufficiently to qualify for ordination in the unusually short time, for one of his Order, of six years. He celebrated his first Mass on the feast of the Annunciation, his natal feast day, which was transferred that year to April 4th. No one would have predicted that two years later, in 1625, this invalid consumptive would make his first voyage to Canada, and, when driven out by the English in 1629, return there in 1633 to become the giant Apostle of the Hurons.

Next to Brébeuf in order of years was Daniel, also Norman, from the seaport of Dieppe, born May 27, 1601. He had finished his rhetoric and philosophy, and was studying law when he decided to become a Jesuit, following Brébeuf in the Rouen novitiate in 1621. After the customary two years he began a four years' term of teaching in the college in that city, leaving there to study theology at Clermont College, Paris. After his ordination to the priesthood in 1631, he taught humanities again in the College at Eu, and then, with Brébeuf, he assisted the rector there until he sailed for the Mission of New France, arriving at Cape Breton in 1632, preceding Brébeuf who was to come back to the mission the year following.

Four years younger than Daniel, Garnier was a Parisian, born on May 25, 1605. He was educated at Clermont, then one of the most notable colleges in France. His parents were rich, but the money they allowed him went for the relief of prison inmates. At nineteen he became a Jesuit, following the usual training courses still at Clermont, then teaching at Eu from 1629 to 1632. Ordained priest three years later, he was assigned to the Canada Mission, but out of consideration for his father who, though a staunch benefactor of the

Jesuits, had reluctantly consented to Charles becoming one of them, his departure was delayed a year. He sailed at length with Jogues in April, 1636.

Paris was the birthplace of Gabriel Lalemant, the last of the Martyrs to reach New France. He was born October 10, 1610. Two of his uncles were distinguished Canadian missionaries, Charles and Jerome. After making his vows as a Jesuit, in Paris, in 1632, he added a fourth vow to devote his life to the Indians. He had to wait fourteen years to fulfil that vow. Meanwhile, he was reviewing his classical studies, reading philosophy, teaching the classics and mastering theology. As priest, owing to weak health he was chaplain for a year at the college of La Flèche. Then he taught philosophy at Moulins for a year and superintended the studies at Bourges from 1644 to 1646, when he embarked for Canada.

Youngest of all these missionaries was Chabanel, born February 2, 1613, in southern France near Mende, soon after the Huguenots had devastated that region. A Jesuit at the age of seventeen, he followed the usual courses of philosophy and theology, teaching between them for an interval of five years. In 1643 he embarked for Canada arriving there on August 15th, after a three months' voyage.

Goupil and Lalande, lay assistants of the missionaries, both died as companions of Jogues. They were called *donnés*, that is, given, or dedicated to their work, oblates as we would style them now, a factor in the success of the priests which we can scarcely appreciate. Goupil was born at Angers, the same year as Jogues. Lalande's birthplace was Dieppe: only that is known of him, and where and how he died so nobly. Goupil tried hard to be a Jesuit and he actually entered the novitiate, but his health forced him to resign. He then studied surgery and found his way to Canada, where he offered his services to the missionaries, matching the most heroic of them by his fidelity, fortitude in suffering and martyrdom.

The Society of Jesus, of which the six priests were members, was then nearing the completion of the first century of its existence. Founded in 1540 by Ignatius Loyola, who had planned to restrict its membership to sixty, in 1615 it numbered 13,112, distributed over thirty-two provinces, with over five hundred and fifty houses, and three hundred and seventy-two of these attached to as many colleges. It was governed from that year until 1645 by Mutius Vitelleschi. Before his death the membership had increased by three thousand, and the number of houses had doubled, the colleges alone exceeding five hundred and twenty-five. It was a time of development in the character and quality of work as well as of membership. Under the previous General, Claudius Acquaviva, the entire body had been so closely organized and its various activities so well regulated, that it could adapt itself to the needs of the time, in missionary as well as in civilized countries, and assume new tasks without impairing the spirit which animated it. To preserve and strengthen this spirit was always a prime consideration with its members as well as with those who were appointed to govern it. To this alone must be ascribed whatever the Society as a whole or its individual members have accomplished.

Whether Brébeuf and Daniel, as well as the other four, came under the influence of this spirit during their college course is not known. Before entering the novitiate they had studied humanities and philosophy, and they were fully prepared for the formation they were to receive. It will be observed that all these young men had finished college when not much older than students finishing in our high school today. Ranke remarks that in the Jesuit schools in Germany of that time, "young people learned more under them in half a year than with others in two years."[10] This was true of the schools in France also. Schwickerath cites testimonies to the excellence of the French Jesuit colleges, and says that nowhere was the Ratio, the Jesuit system of education, better followed than in La Flèche.[11]

As novices their academic studies were interrupted for a while, but this does not mean that their minds were let lie fallow. On the contrary, during that time their mental application was more

systematic and intense than would be required of
them in any school. They were engaged in meditation twice daily, an hour in the morning and a
half-hour in the evening. Daily also they read
books by masters, not only in mystical and ascetical
knowledge, but also in biography, history, and
constantly the Holy Scripture. They were practised in the habit of analysing what they read, and
especially of what they heard in the instructions
given them every day by one skilled in spiritual
matters. They were taught to cultivate a vigilant
and correct conscience. Conversation for them was
not only the art of speaking with one another, but,
in its old and broader meaning, the manner of deal-
ing with everyone, the virtue of modesty, the
Roman moderation, always in control. They had
their times for manual labor, outdoors and indoors,
for walking, for recreation, for games. Perhaps it
was in these that Jogues learned to run swifter
than any Indian. Even in recreation they spoke
a great part of the time in Latin; their books were
in all the modern languages; they received letters
written by Jesuits already employed in every part
of the globe. They visited the hospitals and went
about on pilgrimages, often working their way and
begging bread or lodging. They were trained to
meet privation, hardship and occasional opposition
or humiliation, not stoically, as if such things were
a matter of course, but heroically and in Christian-

like manner, as things good to bear, and to bear like Christ.

The chief factor in the training of a Jesuit is the Spiritual Exercises, the system, or method, as it may be called, of religious formation devised by Ignatius. The name means activity of the soul or spirit, just as manual or physical exercise means activity of the body. This spiritual activity moreover has a very definite purpose. Just as well-regulated bodily exercise fits muscle and nerve, joint and limb to perform various tasks with ease and pleasure, so these spiritual exercises gradually enable the faculties, mental and moral, to accomplish difficult things without failure or fatigue, even with delight. For most people it is irksome and even distasteful to meditate, especially when the object of the meditation is unusual or above their comprehension. They are content with words, without weighing their meaning. God, life, soul, duty, death, are known to them, but not so as to inspire them. Christ is an object of veneration, but more as if He were of the past rather than an animating principle for the present. The Exercises of Ignatius would change all this.

We can imagine these six ardent young men when first they attempted this system of spiritual athletics. They had been brought up piously. They knew much about God and His Divine law, about Christ, the Church, saints, sin and sacraments. Now, however, for the first time they would apply their reason calmly, leisurely, attentively and without emotion, to think of God as Creator, of man as creature endowed with life and faculties for a purpose, and of his consequent obligation to work out that purpose, that is, to serve God as perfectly as possible; to consider this as the essential thing, and all others, health, acquisition of wealth, honor, success, longer or shorter life, as subservient to this. It is one thing to repeat words, or to use them superficially; another to reason profoundly about their meanings, and to think correctly. What effect such reasoning must have will appear later in a Jogues' meek submission to God's will when he was tortured beyond mere human endurance by the Iroquois, or in a Chabanel when urged to give up his missionary career because of insurmountable difficulties, dedicating himself by vow, even though it should involve, as it did not long after, his death.

With a right estimate of God, of His goodness and power, comes a new sense of the enormity of evil, of one's responsibility and guilt in committing it, and of one's own helplessness to overcome it. The Exercises bring this helplessness home, not as it is in others, but in oneself. This is the whole difference between Ignatius as Reformer and the multitude who have won that title by attempting to reform in others what they would not change in themselves. He leads one to realize the need of self-reform, and he points the way to Christ as the only means of achieving this because He is not only the source of Divine grace, but also the model for all genuine reformation. Indeed, reformation is not the ideal to which He would have the soul aspire. It is only a means to an end, and the end is to follow Christ as leader closely, to know Him intimately and to love Him with an affection for which He set the measure — the love greater than which no man can have, even to the laying down of life for a friend — the friend Christ Himself.

Charles Lalemant, the novice-master of Jogues, Brébeuf and Daniel, whose writings are to-day used by those who value real mysticism, must have been delighted with the response of these generous souls as he made known to them the invitation of Christ to help Him establish His Kingdom on earth, and set before them the two standards, that of Christ and that of Satan, not to bid them choose, but to make them more ardently devoted to their Leader, Christ. An appeal to the emotions! Yes, but to emotions stirred by a calm and enlightened reasoning, emotions which no mind can resist that dares reason rightly about Christ. It was this that prepared them for their life's work. Some of them, Gabriel Lalemant, for instance, had become Jesuits with the purpose of becoming missionaries. Here was an appeal to all. The appeal was not to the enchantment of distant lands nor to the romance of adventure, but to the task of preparation, the slow, dull, relentless effort to qualify for fields which needed the spirit of martyrs.

The Exercises animated Jogues and his companions with this martyr spirit, the spirit of an Order which since its foundation has been, like Christ after whom it is named, a sign for contradiction. They knew in France what it was to be the scapegoat, to have the crime of the assassin Ravaillac charged against them; to have the University of Paris and the Parliament of that and other cities arrayed against them; to have been suppressed; to witness their own Biard and Massé go forth in spite of incredible annoyances and obstacles to the very Mission to which they aspired and come back after acting as Confessors of the Faith, only to find their calumniators preceding them. They had no lack of object lessons. Far from being moved by fear, they were inspired to face similar ordeals or worse. This is the characteristic negative effect of the Exercises, the defiance and conquest of fear, of the phobias, to use the slang of the psychology of the day, and the consequent readiness to adopt a course of life regardless of all that usually daunts the human spirit. Free of its fears, the soul is in a position to decide on any noble course, no matter how arduous, and this decision is the culminating act of the Exercises. All that goes before leads up to it, all that follows confirms it. It becomes the turning point of life. It fixes the principles on which one will act for the future and it starts the habits which will characterize one's whole existence. It puts the will, guided by reason, in supremacy over every other faculty and sense. With this habit of decision come the precious habits of initiative, resource, labor, order, system, energy, perseverance. In this way did Jogues, Brébeuf and their future companions in New France pass an entire month early in their novitiate. The experience of this month put a new spirit into their entire after life. The Exercises, true to their title, form not militant Christians only, as some would have it, but genuine athletes of Christ.

After the novitiate Jogues, Chabanel and Garnier received and extended their studies in philosophy for three years. Lalemant, who had studied philosophy for three years, and Daniel for two years, before entering the novitiate, were appointed to teach, Lalemant at Moulins, and Daniel at Rouen. Brébeuf was physically unfit to teach or follow exacting courses of study. Philosophy was a live branch of knowledge in those days, especially in the country in which Descartes, Malebranche and Pascal were influencing thought and in a Society in which the works of Suarez, Vasquez and Molina were then the vogue. It was never a tame study in Jesuit schools, nor one-sided. Every view, system, opinion, school, theory is put before the students, or scholastics, as they are called. They are required not only to recite what they gather from lectures, but to engage in disputation over it before their assembled classes, to write occasional essays on crucial questions and to pass each year oral

examinations in entire treatises. Precision of statement is the chief requirement. No quarter is given
to vague terminology or wandering from the precise
point at issue. As in the Exercises so in the philo-
sophical studies, reason is paramount. Philosophy
was the general term, as it still is in Jesuit schools,
with its divisions of mental philosophy — with sub-
divisions of logic, cosmology, metaphysics, psychology, epistemology, ethics, theology apart from
revelation; and natural philosophy, or science:
mathematics, mechanics, physics, biology, chemis-
try, astronomy. Jogues, and later Lalemant,
passed these three years at La Flèche, the favorite
college of Henry IV, noted for its courses in
mathematics and physics, with its two thousand
students; Garnier was at Clermont; Chabanel at
Toulouse. Daniel and Lalemant had studied
philosophy sufficiently before becoming Jesuits.

All but Brébeuf taught from three to five years
in the colleges of the Order prior to the study of
theology and immediate preparation for the priesthood; Jogues at Rouen, where he was to live with
Brébeuf and Enemond Massé, both already back
from the missions in Canada and hoping to return
thither; Chabanel at Toulouse; Daniel at Rouen;
Garnier at Eu; and Lalemant at Nevers. The
five were engaged in teaching the humanities.
Each had the entire instruction of his class, taking
it as a rule through all the grades up to philosophy,
and associating intimately with his students, in their
recreations, games and pious practices.

CHAPTER THREE

The Missions of New France

A. D. 1608-1614

Exploration of Canada — Religious motive of Cartier and of the French — Voyages, 1534-1543 — Colonization suspended for sixty years — Henry IV, expedition of 1603 — Dissensions over religion—Champlain, ideals as colonizer—Lescarbot; Abbé Fléché — Baptizing uninstructed Indians — Opposition to Jesuits as missionaries for Acadia — Madame de Guercheville — Fathers Biard and Massé — Obstacles to their embarking for New France — de Guercheville comes to their aid — Friction with Biencourt — The new colony at Saint-Sauveur — Argall, abductor of Pocahontas, pirates Acadia — Ill-treatment of missionaries — Return to France — Why missions often seem failures.

ONLY men of hardy fibre would venture overseas in those days to lands where life was far more difficult and beset with peril than it is in Alaska to-day. Prior to the year 1608 none but fishermen and fur-dealers, Breton, Norman and Basque, would go there more or less regularly for their profitable wares, and they only to the coast line, always during milder seasons, and never to remain. A stronger and more disinterested motive was needed to allure men to penetrate a wilderness inhabited by uncivilized peoples, and dwell there during the fierce winters with no thought of returning to the country which was then at the summit of civilization. Such a motive it was that had animated certain French explorers, during the reign

of Francis I, among them Jacques Cartier of Malo
who, when sailing for Canada, hoped to find a
route to India or China, not in quest of new land
or store of wealth, but "to make known the most
sacred name of God and our Holy Mother the
Catholic Church". This was why he requested the
king to provide six chaplains, in addition to the
two hundred and seventy-six passengers he proposed
to take on his third voyage.[12] On previous voyages
in 1534 he had preached to the Indians, whose
language he did not know, gathering them about a
tall cross and pointing from it to the heavens; and
again, in 1535, warning those who lived about
Stadacon, site of the future Quebec, that the god
they invoked "was an evil spirit and that they must
believe only in Jesus Christ".[13] It was the custom
of discoverers in those days, when taking over new
lands, to place in some central spot a symbol of
possession. Cartier's symbol was the Cross.

Reading the story of Cartier's hardships and
mishaps, one wonders that he should have come
back there a third, and again a fourth time. He
had to suffer illness, lack of provisions, discontent
among his followers, not to speak of intense cold
and privation of every sort. His last voyage was
in 1543. He died in 1557. At his death New
France ceased as a colony for sixty years. Every
Frenchman left the country, leaving only among
the Indians their friendly dispositions, inspired by
Cartier's dealings with them. Fisherman and fur-

dealer continued going as before on their very
profitable excursions. Frenchmen, however, were
poor colonizers. There was too much at home to
attract them. Moreover, conditions in France
during the last half of the sixteenth century did
not favor expeditions to other lands.

Henry IV was strongly in favor of re-colonizing
New France, but his minister Sully opposed him.
Among others, Henry had commissioned the
Marquis de La Roche, a Catholic, and Chauvin, a
Protestant trader, to establish in Canada Christianity and New France. It was a strange combination of mixed religions and trade, and the crew
that sailed with them was made up of convicts who
had been condemned to death. Fortunately neither
they nor their descendants remained in Canada.
With this expedition was the Huguenot, de Monts.
In 1603 Aymar de Chastes organized a company
for the purpose of colonizing the new territory, but
he died during the voyage. When Champlain
urged a determined policy for the colonization of
Canada, the king commissioned de Monts to go
there in his name, as successor to Commander de
Chastes. In return for trading privileges, he was
to do all in his power to bring the Indians to a
knowledge of the Christian Faith. Champlain narrates how the crew, a mixture of Catholics and
Huguenots, were in constant conflict over religion,
even priest and minister taking part in it. The
quarrels did not cease on their arrival at Acadia.

There the Indians also took part. When priest and minister died, almost at the same hour, and were buried in one grave, the obsequies did not put an end to the angry disputes among mourners on both sides. Whereupon Champlain remarks that two opposing religions will never do much for the glory of God among infidels they would wish to convert.[14]

De Monts took with him Champlain, a priest Nicholas Aubry, a Protestant minister, and Pontgravé, Baron de Poutrincourt. To obtain money to develop the colony, de Monts organized a company of merchants. To protect their monopoly he took every means to cut off the independent traders, who had hitherto controlled the commodities of New France. Like Cartier, Champlain excelled all this motley company, not only by his experience as navigator and ability as commander, but also by his high and disinterested motives. He had sailed over the central and southern Atlantic, looking for the passage around the globe which all the navigators of his time were seeking. He proposed over three hundred years ago that the passage be made somewhat as has been done in our time by the Panama Canal. He was seeking not to amass wealth or personal advancement, but to transplant to a new world the civilization of his mother country, and the establishment there of the Christian religion. The independent traders whom de Monts had excluded from the colony could oppose his monop-

oly, and they did this so successfully as to have
him recalled. They could not oppose Champlain
with success, as their motives were so far below
his. De Monts, without due authorization it would
seem, had turned over his rights to Poutrincourt,
who was then back in France. Accompanied by
Marc Lescarbot, a lawyer who desired to take part
in the new colony, Poutrincourt returned to Port
Royal, and began at once to put the place in a
prosperous condition. Everything was provided
for, except the ministry of religion. There was no
priest. Lescarbot undertook to act as preacher and
catechist. He has often been called Huguenot, but,
as Goyau points out, in the preface of his translation of Baronius' "Discourse on the Reunion of the
Churches of Russia and Alexandria to the Holy
Catholic Church", he speaks in a manner that leaves
no doubt of his Catholicity.[16] He had the missionary spirit, but he was not an admirer of Jesuits;
he did his best to keep them from New France. The
widow of Henry IV, Marie de Medicis, was bent
on carrying out the king's counsel to Poutrincourt
to have Jesuit missionaries, telling him: "I design
the structure; my son will build it". At the king's
request two Jesuits, Pierre Biard and Enemond
Massé, had been instructed to proceed to Port
Royal in 1608.

Poutrincourt did not want them. He had become prejudiced against Jesuits by hearing the
charges made against them by the Reformers. He

would not provide for their journey to Acadia. While they were waiting for a vessel, he sent a priest from Langres, Abbé Fléché, to Port Royal, with directions to his son Biencourt who was there to hasten the instruction of the Indians, so that some of them might be baptized as soon as possible. It was done. In a few months twenty-one were baptized. Whilst Biencourt was returning to France with the good news, and hoping incidentally to show that the mission could get on without Jesuits, Henry IV was assassinated by Ravaillac. The widowed queen was consoled by Biencourt's report, but she saw in it all the more reason for the Jesuits' hastening to their mission. Biencourt, seeing that he could not prevent them from going, sought to procure passage for them, but then arose another difficulty. The two priests had been generously provided with three thousand livres, by the queen, and with a chapel, complete outfit and every provision for the voyage by Madame de Guercheville and other noble women. This generosity to the missions of New France was to be characteristic of the French, especially of the women, as long as the missions lasted. The owners of the cargo on the vessel, which was to carry the Jesuits to their mission, were Calvinists. They would not consent to taking the Jesuits aboard. Madame de Guercheville started a subscription, obtained enough, four thousand livres, to buy out the owners of the cargo, gave it over to the missionaries, and still received contributions enough to establish a fund which would yield a mission revenue every year. Nothing better in a good enterprise than unreasonable opposition!

It is a matter of surprise to many that missionary effort is often ineffective, or at least slow to produce results. They do not appreciate the difficulties inherent in the missionaries' work, and the obstacles which are too commonly put in their path. The privations, hardships, dangers they must encounter are not by any means their most trying experience. Imagine Biard leaving his chair of theology at Lyons, and Massé giving up his place as assistant to Father Coton at the French Court, to dwell among the Souriquois at Port Royal and the Etchemin Indians across French Bay, and attempt to civilize and teach them Christianity without knowing a word of their language. Here is the first barrier to their great message. Massé goes into the woods to live with the roving bands, and pick up now and then a word of their speech. Biard remains with the few who stay at the settlement, bribing them with food and sweets for the word he needed. After a year they were able to compose a catechism, and begin their lessons to the natives. It was no easy task. These Indians were nomadic, living by fishery and the chase. They were fairly honest, intelligent and docile. The men had several wives and they were not content with that. They were given to drunkenness and sorcery. The Etchemins, about five thousand in number, were averse to Christianity. The Souriquois, less than four thousand, were gentle and more favorable, but they lacked the religious sense. To add to their indisposition, they had got the impression from Biencourt's twenty-one hasty converts and the hundred or more who followed them, that to be baptized meant to become like a Frenchman, without, however, giving up any excess, whether in the number of their wives or of their vices.

The attitude which Biard and Massé had to take toward these ill-instructed converts was a constant source of irritation for Biencourt. Aware of his prejudices against them, they had done everything in their power to conciliate him, but they could not yield on this point. Sensitive about his jurisdiction, now that his father had gone back to France, he resented their insistence on having the Indians who wished to be considered Christian, know and practise their religion. Here was another impediment to the success of the missionaries, from a source whence it should have been least expected.[17]

Meanwhile Biencourt's father was in France, seeking financial aid for the colony. When all others failed him, he had recourse to Madame de Guercheville. She offered to freight a vessel, on the condition of sharing the profits and the lands also, which the king had granted him. He would agree to her receiving part of the profits on the cargo, but no share in the land. Discovering that de Monts still really owned the lands, she obtained title to them and the king confirmed her title to all the land, which at that time was claimed as Acadia, from Florida to the St. Lawrence; Port Royal was excepted. No sooner in possession than she fitted out an expedition, which reached Port Royal late in January with provisions for the colonists, who had all, missionaries included, been living for two months on a week's ration of eleven ounces of bread, a half-pound of lard, three measures of beans, and one of prunes. There was rejoicing, but there was also dishonesty on the part of the leader of the expedition, Simon Imbert, who, when detected, blamed the missionaries. Biencourt at first sides with him. They without difficulty prove Imbert is the culprit. This strains their relations with Biencourt. Madame de Guercheville quickly decides that religion cannot prosper under the control of men who have in view trade and its profits only. She equips liberally a new expedition to establish a colony where the missionaries can have a free hand. Two more Jesuit priests and a lay-brother were among the thirty men led by Saussaye, who arrived at Port Royal March 12, 1613. Biencourt directed them to Mt. Desert, where among the Etchemins the missionaries could labor unhampered, and evangelize also the Abenakis.

The trials of Biard and Massé appeared to be at an end. "It is now our autumn, our harvest time", wrote Biard. Saussaye devoted his energy to planting and sowing, little dreaming that forts would be even more needed than food. Just then in the Virginia colony to the south, the captain of a merchant vessel, Samuel Argall, had brutally abducted Pocahontas and demanded ransom from her father, the Indian chief Powhatan. The father declared war. Argall embarked on his vessel with fourteen cannon and sixty men. Storms drove him up the coast. Friendly Indians, believing he was one of the French, told him of the new colony at Saint-Sauveur, now Penobscot. Short of provisions, his men discontented, intending at first to buy what he needed, but finding the place so open to attack, he opens fire, kills Brother Du Thet, wounds two others, seizes three missionaries, pillages the settlement, sets adrift fifteen of the colonists, among them Massé, without chart or compass, and sails back for Virginia with Biard and Quentin aboard.

Thomas Dale was then the colony's governor. He was a beneficiary of Henry IV.[18] For that reason alone, one might have looked to him for civility, at least, to his venerable prisoners. At first he spoke of destroying them. Then, on the advice of his council, he determined to commission Argall to seize Acadia, and to use the missionaries as guides for the expedition. For refusing to do so, Biard was treated ignominiously. Argall decided to take them back with Quentin to Virginia, to be tried and executed like traitors. Argall's three vessels were separated by a storm. His own reached Virginia; a second was lost; the third, with Biard and Quentin aboard, after a rough voyage of several weeks reached the Azores. Rather than get the captain into trouble with the Portuguese, the two missionaries remained stowaways in the hold for the three weeks the vessel remained at Fayal. On arriving in England, he in return had them well-received, and sent back to France. There they found that calumniators had preceded them, blaming them for the destruction of the colony. That was their reward. They had little difficulty in clearing themselves, and they went back to work, preaching and teaching, waiting quietly for an opportunity to go through the same ordeal again. Is there reasonable ground for surprise at anything that can happen to the missionary? That this apparent failure is really only momentary loss or defeat in the ultimate move to victory is evident constantly in these pages.

Biard and Massé were not satisfied with waiting for an opportunity to return to their mission. Massé retired to La Flèche, where he met a number of ardent young Jesuits whom he inspired with his own zeal, Le Jeune, Ragueneau, Vimont and Charles Lalemant, uncle of the martyr of that name. Biard, at Lyons, writes his account of the mission at Port Royal in such a manner as to disprove the calumnies of the anonymous author of a book on the differences between Biencourt and

its exiled missionaries,[19] and also to arouse the
national interest in New France. Although this
document was not originally one of the series of
the "Jesuit Relations", which will be described in a
later chapter, it is always classed with them. Biard
seized on every opportunity for recommending the
mission there. He died as chaplain of the king's
troops, in 1622. Three years later, his companion
Massé was to return to New France. The piracy
of Argall had interrupted for a time the colonization of Acadia. In God's Providence it was to be
resumed, and to flourish abundantly.

CHAPTER FOUR

Missionaries — Layman, Friar and Jesuit

A. D. 1615–1625

Champlain—The Franciscans in New France—A first horror—
Colonists few—Algonquins, Montaignais—No aid from exploiters
of trade—Friars call for Jesuits—Brébeuf, Massé and Charles
Lalemant in Canada, 1625—Winter hunt with the Montaignais.

HAPPEN what might in New France there was
one man who would not desist from his
efforts to transplant thither the civilization of his
native country. He was not a priest, but he had
the missionary spirit. He was very devout. When
governor, as a means of telling the hours, when
timepieces were few, he introduced the custom of
ringing the Angelus morning, noon and evening.
Civilization for him meant religion as well as social
prosperity and trade. He had witnessed the dis-
asters brought about in Port Royal at the attempt
to make Christianity subservient to barter. Samuel
Champlain kept constantly urging that some good
religious should go to New France and that persons
of means should provide for their expenses. The
Franciscans were ready, and the cardinals and
bishops contributed fifteen hundred livres for their
mission. April 24, 1615, they embarked at Hon-
fleur. In one month they were at Tadoussac, in
time to witness a scene which made them realize
how much needed their services were. The Mon-

taignais tribe of that place had captured two
prisoners from another tribe. They bound them,
bit off their thumbs, burned them with irons, had
the women scalp them, then stoned, and cooked and
ate them. It was the challenge of savagery to
civilization. The Franciscans could not prevent it.
However, what their Founder had done to the wild
beast at Gubbio, they would do for these beasts in
human form.

In June the friars Jamet, Le Caron and Dolbeau
were at Montreal. Jamet saw at once that they
could make little headway with the roving Montaignais and Algonquins, but that they might make
some impression on the stay-at-home Hurons. In
August, Le Caron had penetrated into their lake
country and at Ihonatiria he was dwelling in his
combination cabin and chapel. Like the Jesuits at
Port Royal three years before, they found that the
French colonists needed spiritual care as much as
the Indians. How few Frenchmen there were then
in the colony we can gather from the fact that
between 1608 and 1640 only two hundred and
ninety-six men, women and children had arrived
there, less than ten per year, most of them coming
after 1633, chiefly from Normandy, Le Perche,
Île-de-France, and Aunis. The principal tribes
occupying territory from Quebec to the Huron
country at that time were the Algonquins, and a
special family of them known as the Montaignais.
The Algonquins were everywhere from the coast

to our Middle West, and they ranged from our
Kentucky border as far up as Hudson Bay. They
were the most numerous of the Indian peoples. The
Montaignais were on the lower St. Lawrence.
Biard calculated that of the tribe and family both,
there were not more than four thousand in this
region.[20] Both tribes were improvident, begging,
arrogant, superstitious, drunken, implacable as
enemies, polygamous. The Algonquins were cruel,
treacherous and given to foul language, but had a
certain modesty in manner, simplicity and patience.
The Montaignais were good-natured, peaceable,
hospitable, honest, and contented. There was a
sort of balance between their dispositions and their
habits. The missionaries all agreed that they could
be Christianized if they could be induced to settle
in one place.

The friars could look for little help from the
colonial commercial agents. Their financiers in
France had promised the king to aid the missions,
but they exacted from the agents all they made.
They did not want Canada to be colonized: that
would interfere with their monopoly. Champlain
and the Franciscans were bent on attracting to the
new country as many Frenchmen as possible, who
would clear the forests, build houses, till the soil,
trade honestly and thus give the natives an object
lesson which would recommend the teaching of the
missionaries. Le Caron spent ten months with the
Hurons. Part of the time Champlain was with

him. They argued with the Indians in and out of season. Their only rejoinder was that they could not comprehend what was said to them about the God adored by Christians. They too made it plain that they wished to see first how belief in God and the lives of Christians would make the lot of a people better than their own. With Champlain, Jamet and Le Caron returned to France in 1616, in order to urge the need of peopling New France on the Company of Associates. The Calvinists among these Associates could not see why they should help to send anyone to a new country for the purpose of Catholicizing it. Others of the group cared little for the appeal on behalf of civilizing a land whence they sought only fish and fur. Their monopoly was menaced by the Huguenot settlement which the Prince of Condé had encouraged on the banks of the St. Lawrence. Champlain and the Franciscans failed to move them.

Like the Benedictines of the early Middle Ages, the friars undaunted returned to their mission, determined to do their part for the civilization which others would not promote. They cut the forests and brought the land under, and were soon feeding their household without aid from abroad. They opened a school for the Montaignais at Tadoussac; a college for young Indian boys at Quebec. Several of them they sent to their own schools in France. They were generous beyond their resources and energetic beyond their strength. Champlain, confirmed as lieutenant by the new viceroy, Montmorency, persisted in his endeavors to break the monopoly of the Associates. This he succeeded in doing, but only to have them supplanted by a new company organized by the de Caen brothers, both Huguenot. The fortunes of New France seemed to be bound up with this sect. They managed to control in large measure its trade and to impede its colonization. Had they sought to realize Coligny's dream, they might have established a Protestant France in America. They preferred profit to population. The new company promised, as had other financial groups before them, to promote religion in Canada among natives and colonists, but without performance. They would not even provide for the defence of their own citadel, Quebec, on which all depended for trade as well as security against the inroads of the Iroquois. In vain another Franciscan, Le Bailiff, pleaded with the king to require the de Caen Company to live up to its promises. He recognized the justice of the plea; he ordered the Company to send out every two years six families of laborers, carpenters and masons; but all to no purpose. He was at the time too busily engaged in suppressing Huguenot seditions at home to exact an account from them for the neglect of his ordinances at such a distance.[21]

It was altogether a noble fight that the Franciscans made to minister to the Indians without the resources necessary. Le Caron stuck to his post. There was every reason for discouragement, but that is rarely a Frenchman's temptation. He knew all the difficulties in the way of leading the Indians to adopt Christianity, but he had the wisdom of patience. Some day it would be done. He would do his part. Other Franciscans came, a Sagard who grew enthusiastic over the prospect of winning a new people for Christ; a Viel who was to come to Le Caron's relief, hold the fort at Huronia until aid would come from a new source, and then perish at the hands of those to whom he would give salvation. Knowing they could not provide either men or means enough to make the Indians Christian, they decided to call on the Jesuits, and accordingly Piat was commissioned to invite them into the very territory in which they themselves were working. This was in 1625. That year three Jesuits arrived at Quebec in time to meet the Indian traders from Huronia who had just murdered Viel and his catechist, and thrown them into the rapids at the spot which still bears the name Sault-au-Récollet.

Brébeuf was one of this first group, with Massé and Charles Lalemant. They did not go at once to the Hurons, as they could not trust them at the time. Instead, Brébeuf wintered with the Algonquins, learning their ways and their language. What manner of life this was, we have from one who was to lead it about ten years later and who describes it vividly in one of his famous "Relations". Le Jeune will write in 1634:

"Now, when we arrived at the place where we were to camp, the women, armed with axes, went here and there in the great forests, cutting the framework of the hostelry where we were to lodge; meantime the men, having drawn the plan thereof, cleared away the snow with their snowshoes, or with shovels which they make and carry expressly for this purpose. Imagine now a great ring or square in the snow, two, three or four feet deep, according to the weather or the place where they encamp. This depth of snow makes a white wall for us, which surrounds us on all sides, except the end where it is broken through to form the door. The framework having been brought, which consists of twenty or thirty poles, more or less, according to the size of the cabin, it is planted, not upon the ground but upon the snow; then they throw upon these poles, which converge a little at the top, two or three rolls of bark sewed together, beginning at the bottom; and behold, the house is made. The ground inside, as well as the wall of snow which extends all around the cabin, is covered with little branches of fir; and as a finishing touch, a stretched skin is fastened to two poles to serve as a door, the doorposts being the snow itself. Now let us examine in detail all the comforts of this elegant mansion.

"You cannot stand upright in this house, as much

on account of its low roof as the suffocating smoke;
and consequently you must always lie down, or sit
flat upon the ground, the usual posture of the
savages. When you go out, the cold, the snow,
and the danger of getting lost in these great woods
drive you in again more quickly than the wind, and
keep you a prisoner in a dungeon which has neither
lock nor key.

"This prison, in addition to the uncomfortable
position that one must occupy on a bed of earth,
has four other great discomforts,—cold, heat,
smoke, and dogs. As to the cold you have the snow
at your head with only a pine branch between, often
nothing but your hat, and the winds are free to
enter in a thousand places. . . When I lay down
at night I could study through this opening [in the
roof] both the stars and the moon as easily as if
I had been in the open fields.

"Nevertheless, the cold did not annoy me as
much as the heat from the fire. A little place like
their cabins is easily heated by a good fire, which
sometimes roasted and broiled me on all sides, for
the cabin was so narrow that I could not protect
myself against the heat. . . .

"But, as to the smoke, I confess to you that it
is martyrdom. It almost killed me, and made me
weep continually, although I had neither grief nor
sadness in my heart. It sometimes grounded all
of us who were in the cabin; that is, it caused us
to place our mouths against the earth in order to

breathe. . . . I sometimes thought I was going blind; my eyes burned like fire, they wept or distilled drops like an alembic; I no longer saw anything distinctly, like the good man who said, "I see men walking about like trees"; Mark, viii, 24. I repeated the psalms of my Breviary as best I could, knowing them half by heart, and waited until the pain might relax a little to recite the lessons; and when I came to read them they seemed written in letters of fire, or of scarlet. . . .

"As to the dogs, which I have mentioned as one of the discomforts of the savages' houses, I do not know that I ought to blame them, for they have sometimes rendered me good service. True, they exacted from me the same courtesy they gave, so that we reciprocally aided each other, illustrating the idea of mutual benevolence. These poor beasts, not being able to live outdoors, came and lay down sometimes upon my shoulders, sometimes upon my feet, and as I only had one blanket to serve both as covering and mattress, I was not sorry for this protection, willingly restoring to them a part of the heat which I drew from them. It is true that, as they were large and numerous, they occasionally crowded and annoyed me so much, that in giving me a little heat they robbed me of my sleep, so that I very often drove them away. In doing this one night, there happened to me a little incident which caused some confusion and laughter; for, a savage having thrown himself upon me while asleep, I thought it was a dog, and finding a club at hand, I hit him, crying out, *Aché, Aché*, the words they use to drive away the dogs. My man woke up greatly astonished, thinking that all was lost; but having discovered whence came the blows, "Thou hast no sense," he said to me, "it is not a dog, it is I." At these words I do not know who was the more astonished of us two; I gently dropped my club, very sorry at having found it so near me. . . .

"When I first went away with them, as they salt neither their soup nor their meat, and as filth itself presides over their cooking, I could not eat their mixtures, and contented myself with a few sea biscuit and smoked eel; until at last my host took me to task because I ate so little, saying that I would starve myself before the famine overtook us. . . . It was not Our Lord's will that they should be so long without capturing anything; but we usually had something to eat once in two days, —indeed, we very often had a beaver in the morning, and in the evening of the next day a porcupine as big as a sucking pig. This was not much for nineteen of us, it is true, but this little sufficed to keep us alive. When I could have, toward the end of our supply of food, the skin of an eel for my day's fare, I considered that I had breakfasted, dined, and supped well.

"At first, I had used one of these skins to patch the cloth gown that I wore, as I forgot to bring some pieces with me; but, when I was so sorely pressed with hunger, I ate my pieces; and, if my gown had been made of the same stuff, I assure you I would have brought it back home much shorter than it was. Indeed, I ate old moose skins, which are much tougher than those of the eel; I went about through the woods biting the ends of the branches, and gnawing the more tender bark, as I shall relate in the journal. . . .

"So these are the things that must be expected before undertaking to follow them; for, although they may not be pressed with famine every year, yet they run the risk every winter of not having food, or very little unless there are heavy snowfalls and a great many moose, which does not always happen. . . .

"It remains to me yet to speak of their conversation, in order to make it clearly understood what there is to suffer among these people. I had gone in company with my host and the renegade, on condition that we should not pass the winter with the sorcerer, whom I knew as a very wicked man. They had granted my conditions, but they were faithless, and kept not one of them, involving me in trouble with this pretended magician, as I shall relate hereafter. . . .

. . . ."Suffice it to say, that he sometimes attacked God to displease me; and that he tried to make me the laughingstock of small and great, abusing me in the other cabins as well as in ours.

He never had, however, the satisfaction of inciting our neighboring savages against me; they merely hung their heads when they heard the blessings he showered upon me. As to the servants, instigated by his example, and supported by his authority, they continually heaped upon me a thousand taunts and a thousand insults; and I was reduced to such a state, that, in order not to irritate them or give them any occasion to get angry, I passed whole days without opening my mouth. Believe me, if I have brought back no other fruits from the savages, I have at least learned many of the insulting words of their language. . . So these are some of the things that have to be endured among these people. This must not frighten anyone; good soldiers are animated with courage at the sight of their blood and their wounds, and God is greater than our hearts. One does not always encounter a famine; one does not always meet sorcerers or jugglers with so bad a temper as that one had; in a word, if we could understand the language, and reduce it to rules, there would be no more need of following these barbarians. As to the stationary tribes, from which we expect the greatest fruit, we can have our cabins apart, and consequently be freed from many of these great inconveniences. . . ." [22]

CHAPTER FIVE
The Missionary's Fortune
A. D. 1626-1628

Huron country, route from Quebec—Journey under difficulties—
Hurons, government, beliefs, morals, sorcery—A missionary's
perplexities—English invasion of Canada—French colony de-
populated—Missionaries return to France—Brébeuf signs a vow
in blood.

THE following year Brébeuf went with a
Récollet, de La Roche Daillon, and a fellow-
Jesuit, de Noué, to the Huron country. They had
difficulty getting there, Brébeuf especially, who had
grown so large by this time the Indians feared he
would sink the canoe. Some presents and a good
meal won the Indians over, and he was soon in the
land of his desires. The journey was no pleasure-
trip. The distance from Quebec is not more than
six hundred miles. The trail and water route, however, was fully nine hundred, owing to the need
of avoiding difficult country, and of keeping away
from the Iroquois, who were constantly seeking to
destroy the Hurons. Usually the convoys followed
the St. Lawrence to Montreal, then the La Prairie
River, and next the Ottawa as far as Lake Nipis-
sing, then down the French River to Georgian Bay
and thence to Lake Huron. Le Caron had made
this trip, but he did not describe it as vividly as
Brébeuf. We are fortunate in having his report,

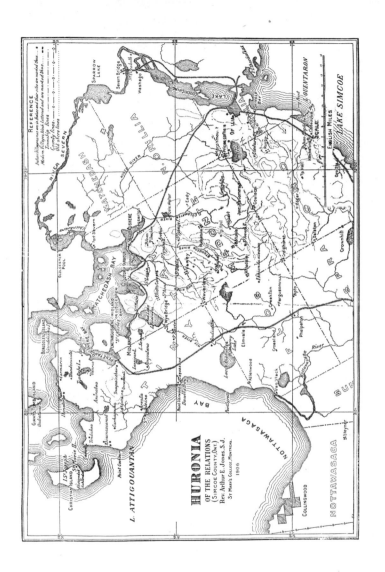

HURONIA
OF THE RELATIONS
(SIMCOE COUNTY, ONT.)
Rev. Arthur E. Jones, S.J.
ST. MARY'S COLLEGE, MONTREAL.
1906

not of this but of a later trip over the same trails and waters. It occurs in his letter to Le Jeune:

". . . Of two ordinary difficulties, the chief is that of the rapids and portages. Your Reverence has already seen enough of the rapids near Kebec to know what they are. All the rivers of this country are full of them, and notably the St. Lawrence after that of the Prairies is passed. For from there onward it has no longer a smooth bed, but is broken up in several places, rolling and leaping in a frightful way, like an impetuous torrent; and even, in some places, it falls down suddenly from a height of several brasses. I remember, in passing, the cataracts of the Nile, as they are described by our historians. Now when these rapids or torrents are reached, it is necessary to land, and carry on the shoulder, through woods or over high and troublesome rocks, all the baggage and the canoes themselves. This is not done without much work, for there are portages of one, two, and three leagues, and for each several trips must be made, no matter how few packages one has. In some places, where the current is not less strong than in these rapids, although easier at first, the savages get into the water, and haul and guide by hand their canoes with extreme difficulty and danger; for they sometimes get in up to the neck and are compelled to let go their hold, saving themselves as best they can from the rapidity of the water, which snatches from them and bears off

[51]

4

their canoe. This happened to one of our Frenchmen who remained alone in the canoe, all the
savages having left it to the mercy of the torrent;
but his skill and strength saved his life, and the
canoe also, with all that was in it. I kept count
of the number of portages, and found that we
carried our canoes thirty-five times, and dragged
them at least fifty. I sometimes took a hand in
helping my savages; but the bottom of the river
is full of stones, so sharp that I could not walk
long, being barefooted.

"The second ordinary difficulty is in regard to
provisions. Frequently one has to fast, if he
misses the caches that were made when descending;
and, even if they are found, one does not fail to
have a good appetite after indulging in them; for
the ordinary food is only a little Indian corn
coarsely broken between two stones, and sometimes taken whole in pure water; it is no great
treat. Occasionally one has fish, but it is only a
chance, unless one is passing some tribe where
they can be bought. Add to these difficulties that
one must sleep on the bare earth, or on a hard rock,
for lack of space ten or twelve feet square on which
to place a wretched hut; that one must endure continually the stench of tired-out savages; and must
walk in water, in mud, in the obscurity and
entanglement of the forest, where the stings of an
infinite number of mosquitoes and gnats are a serious annoyance.

"I say nothing of the long and wearisome silence to which one is reduced, I mean in the case of newcomers, who have, for the time, no person in their company who speaks their own tongue, and who do not understand that of the savages. Now these difficulties, since they are the usual ones, were common to us as to all those who come into this country. But on our journey we all had to encounter difficulties which were unusual. The first was that we were compelled to paddle continually, just as much as the savages; so that I had not the leisure to recite my Breviary except when I lay down to sleep, when I had more need of rest than of work. The other was that we had to carry our packages at the portages, which was as laborious for us as it was new, and still more for others than it was for me, who already knew a little what it is to be fatigued. At every portage I had to make at least four trips, the others had scarcely fewer. I had once before made the journey to the Hurons, but I did not then ply the paddles, nor carry burdens; nor did the other religious who made the same journey. But, in this journey, we all had to begin by these experiences to bear the Cross that Our Lord presents to us for His honor, and for the salvation of these poor barbarians. In truth, I was sometimes so weary that the body could do no more, but at the same time my soul experienced very deep peace, considering that I was suffering for God; no one knows it if he has not experienced it. All did not get off so cheaply." [23]

Daillon settled at Ossossané, the Jesuits at Ihonatiria (at Todd's Point) in the cabin built for the Récollet Le Caron in 1615. De Noué could not master the language; he was too far advanced in years. Without it to remain among the Indians was time wasted. Accordingly, he returned to Quebec, leaving Brébeuf at Ihonatiria. Daillon was soon recalled to Quebec, and Brébeuf was thus entirely alone with the Hurons. He could not gain much headway in his efforts to make them Christians, but he could acquire the knowledge of their language, for which he was celebrated, and he could also study their character and mode of life. What he and others of the missionaries wrote on this subject has come down to us, and it may be thus summarized:

The Hurons were the original stock from which sprung the Iroquois family, Mohawks, Onondagas, Oneidas, Cayugas, Senecas and the Tuscaroras, Cherokees and Andastes. This has been established by all who have studied the derivation of the language of these tribes from that of the Hurons. Their real name was Wyandots, meaning "language [or land] apart". Huron was a nickname given by French sailors who, on meeting some of them at Quebec with their hair furrowed and ridged like a boar's bristles, exclaimed *Quelle hure!* (What boar heads!). At the beginning of the seventeenth century the Hurons dwelt within the Province of Ontario, their main centre being within Simcoe County. To the east and north were the Algonquins, to the south-west the Neutrals and Petuns, or Tobacco Nation. The number of Indians in Huronia in 1636 Brébeuf estimated at about thirty thousand, and the total number of all the tribes, Iroquois included, at more than three hundred thousand. It was not difficult to enumerate them, as they were not a wandering people. It was their settled habit of living that led the missionaries to have great hopes of civilizing and Christianizing them. War and pestilence were continually decreasing their number.

Government, as we know it, was unknown among them. They lived in cabins divided into compartments on either side, like an enlarged sleeping car, a family to each compartment; and in the passage between the compartments a fire-place for every two families. They had councils for deliberation and political decisions, but there was no coercive power. It depended on the leaders, or captains, to persuade the tribesmen to submit to a decision, and on their power of invective to shame the guilty for his misdeeds. They had war chiefs to determine when there should be war and when peace. The affairs of each village, its games, festivals, ceremonies, funerals, were regulated by captains. These were chosen sometimes by election, sometimes by succession. They were all of equal grade: only mental or moral force, especially bravery, entitled any of them to impose his views on the others.

Some of the missionaries, the Récollet Brother Sagard, for instance, and Jerome Lalemant, agreed with Champlain that the Hurons knew no God; that they worshipped a demon or Oki. Sagard was of the opinion that they had a good and bad Oki, and that they believed in a creator Iouskeha, though they did not offer him sacrifice. Brébeuf who lived closest to them concluded that they had a faint and hazy notion of God, but not impressive enough to make them serve or honor Him. They believed that the soul survived the body, but soul for them was not a spiritual substance. They did not look forward to reward or punishment after death. They did, however, fear in this life the displeasure of the great Oki, the power which, in their view, regulated seasons, storms, tempests and other forces. They sought to propitiate this power by throwing tobacco into the flames and pleading for aid, for cures and for other needs. They appeased it by offering the flesh of the victims of violent death. They sacrificed living animals. This confirms Brébeuf's view that they had a perverted notion of God, and that they were a degenerate people who were clinging to the remnant of a revelation their ancestors had once possessed.

The Hurons were depraved and degraded. Vice ran riot among them. They were proud beyond conception, lustful, deceitful, thieving, cruel, brutal, filthy and repulsive. They were treacherous and hypocritical. Lavish in hospitality, they would feast to the full the victim they were to torture like demons as soon as the repast was over. The men wore scarcely anything; the women were covered from shoulder to knee. They held to the principle of marriage to one only, but they violated it in practice by the most promiscuous licence. They were jealous of their traditions, and bound down by tribal customs and conventions. When inclined to follow a better instinct of decency, pity, honor, they were cowed into doing the opposite by fear of the tribal usage and sentiment. They taught their young to cultivate their vices. They believed in sorcery, and practised it incessantly. Indeed they were constantly under the influence of those who pretended to be sorcerers. They were so given over to it, they believed that the missionaries must live by it also. This for many years was the chief obstacle to their conversion to Christianity. Indeed, it was the cause of the martyrdom of many a missionary at the hands of the Iroquois, who believed in it even, if possible, more than the Hurons.[24]

Brébeuf showed extraordinary physical courage in dwelling alone with these people. His moral courage was greater still. Not only did he fail to make any converts among them; he soon discovered that they were suspicious of everything about him.

There was a drought, the crops were withering, and a contagious disease attacked them. They attributed their misfortunes to his presence and the most sacred things in his cabin. The cross on top of the chapel section of his cabin was the particular object of their dread.

The captains of the village, having heard these stories, sent for me and said, 'My nephew, here is what so-and-so says; what dost thou answer to it? We are ruined, for the corn will not ripen. If at least we should die by the hands and arms of our enemies who are ready to burst upon us, well and good,— we should not at any rate pine away; but if, having escaped from their fury, we are exposed to famine, that would be to go from bad to worse. What dost thou think of it? Thou dost not wish to be the cause of our death? besides, it is of as much importance to thee as to us. We are of the opinion that thou shouldst take down that Cross, and hide it awhile in thy cabin, or even in the lake, so that the thunder and the clouds may not see it, and no longer fear it; and then after the harvest thou mayest set it up again.' To this I answered, 'As for me, I shall never take down nor hide the Cross where died He who is the cause of all our blessings. For yourselves, if you wish to take it down, consider the matter well; I shall not be able to hinder you, but take care that, in taking it down, you do not make God angry and increase your own misery. Do you believe in this deceiver?

He does not know what he says. This Cross has been set up for more than a year, and you know how many times there has been rain here since. Only an ignorant person would say that the thunder is afraid; it is not an animal, it is a dry and burning exhalation which, being shut in, seeks to get out this way and that. And then what does the thunder fear? This red color of the Cross? Take away then, yourselves, all those red figures and paintings that are on your cabins. To this they did not know what to reply; they looked at each other and said, 'It is true, we must not touch this Cross; and yet,' added they, '*Tehorenhaegnon* says so.' A thought came to me. 'Since,' said I, '*Tehorenhaegnon* says that the thunder is afraid of this color of the Cross, if you like we will paint it another color, white, or black, or any other; and if, immediately after, it begins to rain, you will be sure *Tehorenhaegnon* has told the truth; but if not, that he is an impostor.' 'Well said,' they replied, 'we will do that.' The Cross was therefore painted white, but one, two, three, four days passed without any more rain than before; and meanwhile all who saw the Cross became angry at the sorcerer who had been the cause of disfiguring it thus. Thereupon I went to see the old men. 'Well, has it rained any more than before? Are you satisfied?' 'Yes,' said they 'we see clearly enough that *Tehorenhaegnon* is only a deceiver; but now, do thou tell us what to do,

and we will obey thee.' Then Our Lord inspired
me to instruct them in the mystery of the Cross,
and speak to them of the honor that was everywhere rendered to it; and to tell them that it was
my opinion that they should all come in a body,
men and women, to adore the Cross in order to
restore its honor; and, inasmuch as it was a matter
of causing the crops to grow, they should each
bring a dish of corn to make an offering to Our
Lord, and that what they gave should afterwards
be distributed to the poor of the village. The
hour is appointed for the morrow; they do not
wait for it, they anticipate it. We surround the
Cross, painted anew in its first colors, upon which
I had placed the Body of Our Lord crucified; we
recite some prayers; and then I adored and kissed
the Cross, to show them how they ought to do it.
They imitated me one after the other, apostrophiz-
ing Our Crucified Savior in prayers which natural
rhetoric and the exigency of the time suggested
to them. In truth, their fervent simplicity inspired
me with devotion; briefly, they did so well that
on the same day God gave them rain, and in the
end a plentiful harvest, as well as a profound
admiration for the Divine power."[25]

Brébeuf did not have to endure these misunder-
standings long. The colony was in distress. The
Merchants' Company had used its monopoly to
impoverish colonizers and natives alike. Charles
Lalemant had gone back to France to implore aid.

He found that already Cardinal Richelieu had revoked the Merchants' charter and instituted the new Company of One Hundred Associates. It was too late. The relief ships they sent out from France were betrayed by David Kerkt and his two brothers, refugees from France, and captured by the English, who were seeking to take advantage of the colony's destitution. After closing the St. Lawrence to all relief from France, they compelled Champlain to surrender, and forthwith missionaries and colonists, all save one family, the Heberts, were forced to return to their country, and Canada became for the first time a British colony.

Brébeuf returned to Rouen, and while there made his final year of probation, the crowning observance of the Jesuit in preparation for his life's work. It was a year of quiet, meditation and of planning the future, not so much of what he hoped to do, but rather of what he hoped to be as an instrument in the hand of God, for his own perfection and for the perfection of others. The year over, he pronounced his last vows. He has left us this extraordinary document of devotion. One would imagine that after his experiences with the Indians he might have turned his thoughts to other fields where the harvest would be more promising. On the contrary, suffering had only whetted his appetite for more. Thus he wrote in his journals: "I have felt an ardent desire to suffer something for Jesus Christ. I fear I shall be refused, because Our Lord has thus far treated me with kindness, whereas I have grieviously offended His Divine Majesty. I shall be more confident of salvation when God will give me a chance to suffer". Then he made this vow:

"Lord Jesus, my Redeemer! You have redeemed me by Your blood and Your most precious death. This is why I promise to serve You all my life in the Society of Jesus, and never to serve any other than Thee. I sign this promise in my blood, ready to sacrifice it all for Thee as willingly as this drop. JEAN DE BRÉBEUF, Soc. J."[26]

His offer was accepted, and he kept his promise.

CHAPTER SIX
Missions and Civilization
A. D. 1632–1634

Failure of Huguenot invasion of New France—Colonization in earnest—Its chief promoter, a Huguenot, become Jesuit—Le Jeune's trumpet call to France—Missions a national reawakening, not a conversion of heathen only—The form of his message, "The Jesuit Relations"—Value as documents of North American history—Incentive to missionaries—Factor in the missions of New France, in the foundation of Canada and of a new people.

ENGLAND'S first possession of Canada was not of long duration. There was genuine regard for treaties among nations in those days, and it was not difficult to prove that England's tenure of the colony was unjust. The Kerkt brothers had seized it by an act of war committed while England and France were at peace. Three months before, these two nations had concluded the Treaty of Susa, agreeing not to intermeddle in one another's affairs, particularly when religion was concerned. England had intermeddled to assist the Huguenots, sending ninety vessels with 10,000 troops to La Rochelle to strengthen the uprising of 1627 in the south of France. Richelieu prevented the approach of this fleet, forced the Huguenot stronghold to surrender, and by 1629 had put an end to the political power of the Huguenots and to all strife on the score of religion in France.

The Kerkt seizure of Canada had been prompted by a desire to wrest the colony from its Catholic owners. The Kerkts were of French birth, from Dieppe. To their vice-admiral, Jacques Michel, Jesuits were "dogs from St. Malo". They had acted for England, as England had attempted to aid their fellow-revolutionists in France. The attempt a failure, and the revolution at an end, the question arose, would France reclaim Canada? The Court was not keen on the subject. The people knew too little about it to be interested. Champlain was determined that the colony must come back to its rightful owner. Single-handed at London he pleaded his cause and won. In 1632 England yielded, and he then pleaded with Louis XIII and Richelieu to give once more to the restored territory the light of faith and to confirm their possession of it by an effective colonization.

The way was now clear. No longer would trade or differences over religion be an obstacle. The exploiting company of the de Caens was no more; the Huguenots could no longer impede the work of the missions. The traders had discouraged immigration; the sectarians had fostered dissension on grounds of religion. Henceforth the colony was to be populated by those who would Christianize the Indians, and so far only the Catholics had earnestly attempted this. The Franciscans were invited to return, but they had not men enough for this purpose and very many were needed. Accordingly the Jesuits resumed labors there.

By a strange irony the one who was to do most

to re-establish the missions, and even to develop the colony, had himself been a Huguenot until on attaining his majority he became a Catholic and soon after a Jesuit. He was a man of extraordinary ability, and it was not confined to purely ecclesiastical activity. As superior of the mission he, as a rule, did first what he was afterwards to require from others. The difficulty of learning the Indian tongues was the chief obstacle in the way of the missionaries, particularly for Le Jeune. To master it, as described in the preceding chapter, he spent his first winter among them on their hunt, braving cold and every possible hardship, even famine, in order to overcome this obstacle to his work. He was a man of great spirit. Not only did he appreciate the need of colonization in New France on a large scale, as others — Cartier, Champlain and the Franciscans — had urged it before him; he was able so to impress it on all France as to arouse the interest of the entire French people. Reading his views on Canada, one realizes that he had already conceived the Canada of the present day. He was a political economist, a wise counsellor, and an efficient executive not only in the affairs of his own religious society, but in State affairs as well. According to Kingsford,[27] as Champlain neared his end, Le Jeune was appointed to act as governor in case of emergency. He was also authorized to deliver to Champlain's temporary successor Brasdefer, Sieur de Chasteaufort, his commission as

Governor. The Queen Mother, Anne of Austria, expressed the wish seventeen years later that Le Jeune might be named the first bishop in the new country. In his broad view, the Mission was not merely a task for a body of priests and of their immediate assistants and patrons or supporters. It was an enterprise in which the whole French nation should be concerned. It was not merely for the spiritual benefit of the Indians, but for the spiritual benefit of every man, woman and child in France. It was a means destined by God to create a new spirit of faith and of fervor; to inspire a whole people with new ideals; to arouse them to contribute, not their money only, but their very souls. Court and cloister and countryside were called on to look beyond geographical horizons, to rise above a false patriotism which kept the nation from expanding and diffusing the gifts, spiritual and material, which it possessed in plenty.[28]

Le Jeune arrived in New France in 1632. Soon after came Anthony Daniel in the ship of which his brother Charles was captain. They remained for a while at the new fort near Cape Breton. By the time the governor, Champlain, arrived with Brébeuf and Massé, in 1633, Le Jeune was ready not only with his programme but with his plan of campaign. It was very simple. As Goyau remarks, he was not one to leave to God what he could do himself.[29] He was a man of ways and means as well as of large views. Others had seen as clearly

as he what was needed, like Biard and Sagard.
They had even exposed these needs in book and
pamphlet, as did the Franciscan Le Bailiff and the
Jesuit Noyrot, in conferences with king and
minister. Their writings reached only a few, and
long after the happenings they narrated. Some
of them, Lescarbot for instance, appealed to a
partisan element, and could not therefore evoke
a general sentiment. Le Jeune conceived the plan
for keeping the entire nation informed of actual
conditions and affairs in New France precisely as
they were, without delay and always so vividly as
to capture the imagination of his readers, hold their
interest, and convince them that they were profoundly concerned in all he said. His first story
of his experiences, of his voyage to the new country, of the storms he encountered, of a great catch
of cod-fish over the deck on Pentecost, of his meeting the Indians with painted faces at Tadoussac,
of his attempt to rescue Indian prisoners, of their
torture, of his own rescue from drowning in the
St. Lawrence, all written and despatched to France
within two months, and published before the end
of the year, was in that day what a radio message
from the earth's end is in our own. The effect was
electric. His words were not merely a news report;
they were a summons to action. The response was
immediate and, characteristic of Frenchmen, it was
also generous and enthusiastic.

"Shall the French alone of all the nations of

the earth, be deprived of the honor of expanding and spreading over this New World? Shall France, much more populous than all the other kingdoms, have inhabitants only for herself? When her children leave her shall they go here and there and lose the name of Frenchmen among foreigners?"[30]

Year after year these reports and appeals were to go from Canada to France. The first nine years Le Jeune was to write them, often embodying with his own the writings of various Jesuits, Brébeuf, Perrault and others. They are known as the "Jesuit Relations".[31] Their influence then and their importance still as documentary sources for all who write about North America, its missions and its martyrs, are a subject of never-ceasing interest. Jesuit missionaries had always made it a point to write from their distant stations accounts of their labors in strange fields and of the character and habits of the peoples they sought to enlighten. Saint Francis Xavier was the first to recommend to his associate, Joam Beira, to send to Ignatius in Rome, and to Rodriguez in Lisbon, "such news as when known in Europe would make everyone that heard it give glory to God".[32] His own letters did arouse all Europe, and they still inspire the missionary, Protestant as well as Catholic, to perseverance and self-sacrifice.

The letters of the missionaries of New France were of three kinds. Some were very familiar and personal, addressed to a relative, a friend, a

superior, or to the Rev. Father General, and were
not to be given publicity at that time, if indeed it
could properly be done at any other time; at most,
it was permissible to the person to whom they were
written to communicate them to a circle of discreet
friends, or to make public some inoffensive extracts.
Others, destined only for the members of the
Society of Jesus, were, in the beginning, sent in
manuscript to the different houses of the Order.
They served as a bond between the religious of the
Society, and kept them in touch with the works of
the apostolate, wherever it was carried on. Later
on, the letters of the missionaries were printed, but
after revision and correction, and even translation
into Latin, extracts and analyses were also made,
which were put in a volume, entitled: "Annual
Letters of the Society of Jesus to the Fathers and
Brothers of the Same Society". When the publication of the annual letters ceased in 1654, the
provinces and missions of the Society continued to
write and address them to the Father General.
Many are still being brought to light, especially
relating to New France. There was a third sort of
letters, those which the missionaries wrote for the
public and were intended for publication; these were
generally called "Relations". Such are the "Relations of New France", whose long series open with
that of Biard, in 1616, followed by the
"Relations" of Charles Lalemant, in 1626. The
series from 1632 to 1672 consists of forty-one

volumes, of which thirty-nine bear the title of "Relations", and two (1654–55 and 1658–59) that of "Letters". Other "Relations" exist, likewise written for the public, but never printed.

It is evident that the contents of these various classes of letters must differ according to the purpose of the writer and the character of the receiver. Prudence, discretion and charity would naturally forbid the putting down in black and white for general reading what might, however, with perfect propriety be laid before a superior or a friend. It was not the part of the missionary to publish his views on political matters concerning the government of the colonies, though it would be his duty to warn his superior of past or future complications which concerned the temporal as well as the spiritual welfare of his mission. Hence Le Jeune well remarks: "I do not undertake to record all that takes place in this country; but only what concerns the Faith and religion." From this very fact some critics have arraigned the writers of the "Relations" for the incompleteness of their writings, without taking into account the scope which the Fathers had laid down for their guide. This characterizes the "Relations" not only of Canada, but those of China and Japan as well. The missionaries had in view the edification of their readers; they, therefore, recorded the progress of Christianity, the heroic labors and combats of those engaged in these vast mission fields. They kept silence about many things that would not have served for edification, yet without ever departing from the strict truth. Incomplete, then, as the "Relations" intentionally are, the best judges, Protestant as well as Catholic, pronounce them to be of inestimable value for the history of our country, of certain periods of which they are the sole records.

Parkman writes: "The 'Relations' of the Jesuits appeal equally to the spirit of religion and the spirit of romantic adventure. . . . They hold a high place as authentic and trustworthy documents".[32] No doubt Parkman himself was inspired and encouraged by the heroic lives of the missionaries to labor as he did, in spite of his grievous infirmity. Bancroft, whose own work shows an intimate knowledge of the history contained in the "Relations", says that "the history of the Jesuit Mission is connected with the origin of every celebrated town in the annals of French America. Not a cape was turned, not a river entered, but a Jesuit led the way".[34] Kip remarks that: "There is no page in our country's history more touching and romantic than that which records the labors and sufferings of the Jesuit missionaries." Field writes that: "these 'Relations', for many years looked upon through the haze of sectarian distrust, were lightly esteemed by the students of American history, but the more their character and statements were investigated, the more important and valuable they appeared. They have become the sources from

which we must draw almost all the historic material
of New York and Canada during the first century
and a half of their exploration by Europeans".[35]

Reuben Gold Thwaites, in his estimable collection "The Jesuit Relations and Allied Documents,"
bears the following testimony: "The authors of
the journals which formed the basis of the 'Relations' were, for the most part, men of trained
intellect, acute observers, and practised in the art
of keeping records of their experiences. They had
left the most highly civilized country of their times,
to plunge at once into the heart of the American
wilderness, and attempt to win to the Christian
faith the fiercest savages known to history. To
gain these savages, it was first necessary to know
them intimately — their speech, their habits, their
manner of thought, their strong points and their
weak. These first students of the North American
Indian were not only amply fitted for their undertaking, but none have since had better opportunity
for its prosecution. They were explorers, as well
as priests. . . .

"Many of the 'Relations' were written in Indian
camps, amid a chaos of distractions. Insects
innumerable tormented the journalists, they were
immersed in scenes of squalor and degradation, overcome by fatigue and lack of proper sustenance,
often suffering from wounds and disease, maltreated
in a hundred ways by hosts who, at times, might
more properly be called jailers; and not seldom had

savage superstition risen to such a height, that to
be seen making a memorandum was certain to arouse
the ferocious enmity of the band. It is not surprising that the composition of these journals of
the Jesuits is sometimes crude; the wonder is, that
they could be written at all. Nearly always the
style is simple and direct. Never does the narrator
descend to self-glorification, or dwell unnecessarily
upon the details of his continual martyrdom; he
never complains of his lot; but sets forth his
experiences in phrases the most matter-of-fact.
His meaning is seldom obscure. We gain from his
pages a vivid picture of life in the primeval forest,
as he lived it; we seem to see him upon his long
canoe journeys, squatted amidst his dusky fellows,
working his passage at the paddles, and carrying
cargoes upon the portage trail; we see him the butt
and scorn of the savage camp, sometimes deserted
in the heart of the wilderness, and obliged to wait
for another flotilla, or to make his way alone as
best he can. Arrived at last, at his journey's end,
we often find him vainly seeking for shelter in the
squalid huts of the natives, with every man's hand
against him, but his own heart open to them all.
We find him, even when at last domiciled in some
far-away village, working against hope to save the
unbaptized from eternal damnation; we seem to see
the rising storm of opposition, invoked by native
medicine men — who to his seventeenth-century
imagination seem devils indeed — and at last the

bursting climax of superstitious frenzy which sweeps him and his before it. Not only do these devoted missionaries — never, in any field, has been witnessed greater personal heroism than theirs — live and breathe before us in the 'Relations'; but we have in them our first competent account of the Red Indian at a time when relatively uncontaminated by contact with Europeans."[36]

Dr. Finley in his charming compilation, "The French in the Heart of America", tells us:

"The 'Relations' of the Jesuits are among our most precious chronicles in America. With these the history of the north — the valleys of the St. Lawrence, the Great Lakes, and the Mississippi — begins. The *coureurs de bois* may have anticipated the priests in some solitary places, but they seldom made records. Doubtless, like Nicolet, they told their stories to the priests when they went back to the altars for sacrament, so that even their experiences have been for the most part preserved. But when we know under what distracting and discouraging conditions even the priest wrote, we wonder, as Thwaites says, that anything whatever has been preserved in writing. . . . 'I know not', says one of these apostles in an epistle to the Romans (for this particular letter went to Rome), 'I know not whether your Paternity will recognize the letter of a poor cripple, who formerly, when in perfect health was well known to you. The letter is badly written, and quite soiled, because, in addition to other inconveniences, he who writes it has only one whole finger on his right hand; and it is difficult to avoid staining the paper with the blood which flows from his wounds, not yet healed; he uses arquebus powder for ink, and the earth for a table.' "[37]

The "Relations" are not merely annual reports, or dry records, but intimate revelations of life, the story of civilized men lodging, eating and consorting with peoples who were as savage as have ever been known. As one of their writers, Chaumonot, remarks, they had to be written clandestinely, and carried secretly also to their destination as the Indians given to sorcery looked upon writing as magic and feared it meant harm for them. They are a contribution not only to history but a most important source of ethnography. In fact, as the missionaries of the Society of the Divine Word are proving in our own day, for real knowledge in this science the missionary has the best opportunity, since he knows the language and gradually gets the confidence of the natives. The Jesuits in New France made the most of this opportunity. Their observations are completely and systematically set forth in "Les Mœurs des Sauvages", by Lafitau, whose own personal observations in this field were guided by Charles Garnier.[38]

Could the laudatory extracts already given leave any room for doubt as to the merit of the "Relations," the zeal which book-collectors and historians have shown, during the last half-century, in hunting after original copies, and the expense to which they have gone in purchasing these, or even for publishing reprints of them, are proofs of sincere esteem of them, which the most sceptical cannot question. Thwaites gives a most careful account of the various series of these publications by Dr. R. B. O'Callaghan, Gilmary Shea, and Rev. Felix Martin; also of the reprint of the Cramoisy series in three stout volumes by the Canadian Government in 1858.[39] Throughout his own seventy-three volumes are found valuable information about libraries and collectors who are in possession of the complete edition or of one or more copies of the originals, and also about the prices paid for them.

One need read only a page of these "Relations" picked at random to come under their spell. To stop reading requires an effort. The fascination is lasting. They have been the delight and the incentive of missionaries ever since they were written. They inaugurated a new literature. "The Edifying Letters" of the Jesuits, the "Annals of the Propagation of the Faith" and the numerous missionary periodicals of our day are to a great extent patterned on them.

Immediately on their appearance began the immigration from France which was to be the origin of a new people. Le Jeune had been happy on his return to Quebec to find in the colony the family of Hebert, whose widow, now married to

Guillaume Hubou, was already grandmother. They were practically the only Canadian family left, and they too had thought of leaving but remained in expectation that the missionaries would return. The priest celebrated Mass in their home and chanted a Te Deum.[40] One can imagine his happiness two years later on receiving forty new-comers from Le Perche and another group a year later. Le Perche alone was to send five hundred families to Canada in the next thirty years. Normandy would vie with Le Perche. The tide once started would flow in that direction until the middle of the following century. The stock was of the best. The new arrivals were not political or religious malcontents seeking other shores to practise a greater intolerance than that to which they had been subject at home. Among them was Jean Bourdon, engineer, who was later to be attorney-general for New France and to accompany Jogues on his second journey to the Iroquois country as an ambassador of peace. Abbé Le Sueur was also one of them, the first secular priest in Canada. With Montmagny came the Norman families of Le Gardeur and Le Neuf, Catherine de Cordé with two sons and daughter and Jeanne Le Marchant with two daughters and two sons.[41]

France was actively interested. Young Indians were sent over to its schools. Religious communities petitioned for some to instruct and baptize with marked ceremonies, members of the nobility gladly acting as godparents. The court itself received similar object lessons, and many a story has grown out of the experiences of the naïve children of nature adopted for a time into the advanced civilization of France. The vision flashed on the eyes of France attracted spirits of the highest order. Madame Martin was among the first of these — Venerable Marie de l'Incarnation, as she has been styled. She will lead over the Ursulines who will become like guardian angels to the Indians and to the colonists at Quebec. Madame de La Peltrie will follow. From Dieppe will come three Daughters of Mercy to look after sick colonists. Le Jeune's appeal had been heard. New France through him had its mission for France, as the older country had for the new. Meantime, he and his fellow missionaries with Abbé Le Sueur had been working among Indians and immigrants; of the former he would report twenty-two baptized in 1635, one hundred and fifteen in 1636, and three hundred in 1637.[42] The harvest was slender, but at least the soil had yielded to cultivation and was beginning to bear.

Ioannes de Brebœuf pre Ies

CHAPTER SEVEN
An Apostle and His Mission
A. D. 1634–1636

Brébeuf greets the Hurons at Quebec—They visit his chapel, feast and return to Huronia without him—A year of ministry and patience—Return to Ihonatiria in 1634—Ill-treatment on the way—Huron cabins unlike the Louvre—Assembly and catechism—Zeal unrewarded—Caution in admitting converts—Children the hope of the Mission—The seminary for them in Quebec.

B RÉBEUF, with Massé, had arrived at Quebec June 5th. He began at once to renew his practice in the tribal languages, going out among the Indians usually to visit the sick. On July 28th the Hurons came for their annual market. This year they were more numerous than ever, forty canoes, with sixty of their captains, bent on greeting their friend the new governor, and on resuming relations with the French. With the English they had not been on good terms. They built their cabins, bartered their goods with the French agents, feasted, and then the captains assembled in council to hear Champlain's message to them. Brébeuf spoke to them in Huron to their great delight. He led them to the chapel. That casual visit showed how next to impossible was the task of teaching them the truths of faith. When they were shown more than one statue of the Blessed Virgin, and were told she was the Mother of Our Lord, they wondered how anyone could have several mothers. When they saw the dove representing the Holy Spirit, they said it was the cause of thunder, which they believed was the cry of a huge wild bird. The picture of the flames of hell appealed to them. They believed in some state of existence after death, and they could grasp how one would be either happy or unhappy in that state. It was on this fact, therefore, the missionaries would have to insist later, not however neglecting other truths or facts. Parkman is impatient with them for working on the fears of the Indians, though Christ Himself had appealed to mankind through fear as well as other passions. Champlain fêted the visitors. For them a feast was a gorge. Sagard described one of these feasts for a very much smaller group: fifty-six Canada geese, thirty mallard, twenty teal-duck and a quantity of other game—the quarry of a three days' chase—two barrels of peas, one of sea-biscuit, twenty pounds of prunes, six baskets of Indian corn—all cooked together in the big cauldron of the colony's brewery. It would take a long time for the missionaries to train such people to moderation.

Daniel and Davost had come to Quebec from the fort on St. Anne's Bay near Cape Breton, where they had been attending to the garrison stationed there by Daniel's brother Charles. The Hurons wanted to take them with Brébeuf back to Huronia. Each captain strove for the honor of having a missionary at his own village. All was ready for the journey when an Ottawa captain, Borgne, protested.

Champlain having rejected his plea for the release of a prisoner from a neighboring tribe who had been convicted of murdering a Frenchman, Borgne pretended that the tribe would be so incensed they would destroy the Black Robes, blame this on the Hurons, and start a feud between them and the French. The Hurons were frightened. They declined to take the Fathers, although Brébeuf said they were ready for death and would have no one suffer for their execution. Nothing could change the decision. Brébeuf, therefore, and his companions, greatly disappointed, had to wait for another opportunity. They waited fully a year, Brébeuf active among the neighboring Indian tribes, his companions studying the language and doing what missionary work they could among the Indians about Quebec. It required no slight patience to think of the Huron field waiting to be sown and still be excluded from it. They knew, however, that spiritual seed-time and harvest are not measured by the brevity and regularity of plant and flower, nor by the same proportion as between the sower's labors and his fruits. One of the sublime traits of these men is their confidence, in spite of their own poor results, that one day this wilderness would flourish and blossom like the lily.

Next year no more than seven canoes came down, and they ventured only as far as Tadoussac, but the three priests were there to meet them. Shortly before that, two hundred braves had been killed and two hundred taken prisoners by the fierce peoples of the south, the Iroquois, and the Hurons were downcast. They feared more than ever to take the responsibility of harboring the Fathers, now that the Iroquois might overtake and destroy them. Their fears were quickly quieted by the assurances of the three who were so eager to begin the work to which they had looked forward for years. So eager were Daniel and Davost that they actually left behind their outfits and even the money (beads, etc.) that would help them with the Indians, carrying only their altar-ware and vestments. They started, Brébeuf in one canoe, Daniel and Davost in another. With them were three Frenchmen, who later became companions to the missionaries, Pierre, Martin and Baron. Usually the journey took thirty days. The ordinary hardships of it have been described in the previous chapter. This is Brébeuf's account of the extraordinary sufferings they had to undergo, owing to the meanness of their guides, although, before starting, Daniel, seeing that these had received nothing, had them rewarded with cloaks such as the Indians in the boats had received. It was characteristic of Daniel to give trouble to no one and to see that all were properly considered.

"Father Davost, among others, was very badly treated. They stole from him much of his little belongings. They forced him to throw away a small steel mill, almost all our books, some linens, and a good part of the paper that we were taking, and of which we have great need. They abandoned him at the island of the Alumettes among the Algonquins, where he suffered very keenly. When he reached the Hurons, he was worn-out and dejected, and for a long time he did not recover.

"Father Daniel was abandoned, and forced to seek another canoe, as also was Pierre, one of our men. Young Martin was very roughly treated, and at last left behind with the Bissiriniens, where he remained some time, spending about two months on the road, and arriving among the Hurons only on the nineteenth of September.

"Baron was robbed of his things the very day he arrived in these parts; and he would have lost much more if he had not frightened them with his arms, to give him back some things. In short, all the Frenchmen suffered great hardships, incurred great expense, considering what little they had, and ran serious risks. Whosoever comes here must be prepared for all this, and something more, even death itself, whose image is every moment before our eyes. Not knowing how to swim, I once had a very narrow escape. As we were leaving the Bissiriniens, while shooting a rapid we would have gone over a high falls, had not my savages promptly and skillfully leaped into the water to turn aside the canoe which the current was sweeping. Very likely the others might relate as much, and more, so numerous are such incidents." [43]

Brébeuf narrates how the Indians wanted to
hide somewhere a box belonging to his lay companions; how the Algonquins tried to detain him
at their villages; how the captain of his canoe
wanted to abandon him. He offered to carry
the box they objected to carrying. Daniel was
shipwrecked twice. Baron was marooned, but the
captain of the island insisted that his canoe company should take him with them. The Indians
landed Brébeuf at Toanche, near Thunder Bay,
practically abandoning him. He had to hide his
luggage and wander about until at night he came
to the new site of the village of Ihonatiria. He
knew human nature, and his knowledge was kindly.
"I attribute", he writes, "all these extraordinary
difficulties to sickness among our savages. For we
know very well how sickness alters the disposition
and the inclinations of even the most sociable."

The first need of the missionaries was a cabin
and this the Indians built for them. As Parkman
remarks of the cabin made for Le Jeune at Quebec,
this cabin was the cradle of the great Jesuit missions among the Hurons. Here is Brébeuf's description of it:

"The cabins of this country are neither Louvres
nor palaces, nor anything like the buildings of our
France, not even like the smallest cottages. They
are, nevertheless, somewhat better and more commodious than the hovels of the Montagnais. I
cannot better express the fashion of the Huron

dwellings than to compare them to bowers or garden arbors—some of which, in place of branches and vegetation, are covered with cedar bark, some others with large pieces of ash, elm, fir, or spruce bark; and although the cedar bark is best, according to common opinion and usage, there is, nevertheless, this inconvenience, that they are almost as susceptible to fire as matches. Hence arise many of the conflagrations of entire villages; and, without going farther than this year, we have seen in less than ten days two large ones entirely consumed, and another, that of Louys, partially burned. We have also once seen our own cabin on fire; but, thank God, we extinguished it immediately. There are cabins or arbors of various sizes, some twelve feet in length, others of ten, others of twenty, of thirty, of forty; the usual width is about twenty-four feet, their height is about the same. There are no different stories; there is no cellar, no chamber, no garret. It has neither window nor chimney, only a miserable hole in the top of the cabin, left to permit the smoke to escape. This is the way they built ours for us.

"The people of Oënrio and of our village were employed at this, by means of presents given them. It has cost us much exertion to secure its completion, not only on account of the epidemic, which affected almost all the savages, but on account of the connivance of these two villages; for although the work was not great, yet those of our village followed the example of those of Oënrio, who, in hopes of finally attracting us to their village, simply amused themselves without advancing the work. We were almost into October before we were under cover. As to the interior, we have suited ourselves; so that, even if it does not amount to much, the savages never weary of coming to see it, and, seeing it, to admire it. We have divided it into three parts. The first compartment, nearest the door, serves as an ante-chamber, as a storm door, and as a storeroom for our provisions, in the fashion of the savages. The second is that in which we live, and is our kitchen, our carpenter shop, our mill, or place for grinding the wheat, our refectory, our parlor and our bedroom. On both sides, in the fashion of the Hurons, are two benches which they call *endicha*, on which are boxes to hold our clothes and other little conveniences; but below, in the place where the Hurons keep their wood, we have contrived some little bunks to sleep in, and to store away some of our clothing from the thievish hands of the Hurons. They sleep beside the fire, but still they and we have only the earth for bedstead; for mattress and pillows, some bark of boughs covered with a rush mat; for sheets and coverings, our clothes and some skins do duty. The third part of our cabin is also divided into two parts by means of a bit of carpentry which gives it a fairly good appearance, and which is admired here for its novelty. In the one is our little chapel, in which we celebrate every day holy Mass, and we retire there daily to pray to God. It is true that the almost continual noise they make usually hinders us,—except in the morning and evening when everybody has gone away,—and compels us to go outside to say our prayers. In the other part we put our utensils. The whole cabin is only thirty-six feet long, and about twenty-one wide. That is how we are lodged, doubtless not so well that we may not have in this abode a good share of rain, snow and cold. However, as I have said, they never cease coming to visit us from admiration, especially since we have put on two doors, made by a carpenter, and since our mill and our clock have been set to work." [44]

In the new cabin Brébeuf gave lessons in Huron to his two associates. He writes that they were apt pupils, especially Daniel, who knew more words than Brébeuf himself, but could not connect them promptly.[45] Soon Daniel had the Our Father in Huron, and could lead the children chanting it when Brébeuf had his assembly of the tribe in the chapel of the cabin, at which he preached and recited the prayers. He preached on faith, immortality, heaven and hell. In return he was invited to the Indian assemblies. He became very popular, especially when, after a nine days' prayer he had advised, rain fell and watered the soil. His importance was increased when Champlain sent him letters constituting him his representative among the

Hurons. Daniel went in and about the cabins teaching the children, whether baptized or not, Christian Doctrine. This was the method of teaching it when the people were assembled in the cabin:

"We gave the instruction of catechism in our cabin, for we had as yet no other suitable church. This is often the most we can do; for their feasts, dances, and games so occupy them that we cannot get them together as we would like.

"The usual method that we follow is this: We call together the people by the help of the captain of the village, who assembles them all in our house as in council, or perhaps by the sound of the bell. I use the surplice and the square cap, to give more majesty to my appearance. At the beginning, we chant on our knees the Pater Noster, translated into Huron verse. Father Daniel, as its author, chants a couplet alone, and then we all together chant it again; and those among the Hurons, principally the little ones, who already know it, take pleasure in chanting it with us, and the others in listening. That done, when every one is seated, I rise and make the Sign of the Cross for all; then, having recapitulated what I said the last time, I explain something new. After that we question the young children and the girls, giving a little bead of glass or porcelain to those who deserve it. The parents are very glad to see their children answer well and carry off some little prize, of which they render themselves worthy by the care they take to come privately to get instruction. On our part to arouse their emulation, we have each lesson retraced by our two little French boys, who question each other,—which transports the savages with admiration. Finally the whole is concluded by the talk of the old men, who propound their difficulties, and sometimes make me listen in my turn to the statement of their belief.

"We began our catechizing by this memorable truth, that their souls, which are immortal, all go after death either to paradise or to hell. It is thus we approach them, either in public or in private. I added that they had the choice, during life, to participate after death in the one or the other,— which one, they ought now to consider. Whereupon one honest old man said to me, "Let him who will, go to the fires of hell; I want to go to heaven"; all the others followed and making use of the same answer, begged us to show them the way, and to take away the stones, the trees, and the thickets therein, which might stop them.

"Our Hurons, as you see, are not so dull as one might think them; they seem to me to have rather good common sense, and I find them universally very docile. Nevertheless, some of them are obstinate, and attached to their superstitions and evil customs. These are principally the old people; for beyond these, who are not numerous, the rest know nothing of their own belief. We have two or three of this number in our village. I am often in conflict with them; and then I show them they are wrong, and make them contradict themselves, so that they frankly admit their ignorance, and the others ridicule them; still they will not yield, always falling back upon this, that their country is not like ours, that they have another God, another paradise, in a word, other customs." [46]

A great drought parched the land and threatened famine. The Indians were in despair. Their sorcerers were impotent. The captains besought Brébeuf for relief. He bade them pray, and he opened a nine days' prayer in honor of the mission's patron, St. Joseph. The prayer was favored by abundant rains. Late in that year, 1636, he consecrated the mission to the Blessed Virgin under the title of Immaculate, over two hundred years before the Church pronounced this prerogative as a point of Catholic faith. The Indians were impressed by all this piety, but the older members of the tribe stuck fast to their pagan traditions; the middle-aged were indifferent and too fickle to admit to baptism. Unfortunate as the hasty baptism of the Acadians was under Biencourt, it had the good effect of confirming the Jesuits in the determination to confer baptism on adults only after mature preparation and proof of constancy. The sick near death, old or young, the Fathers would baptize, but no others. Since epidemics were frequent, such baptisms were also frequent. This accounts for the low number of baptisms of adults in good health in the early days of their ministry, but it also accounts for the steadfastness and rare examples of Christian virtues on the part of those who were finally adjudged worthy of the sacrament.

The children were the hope of the missionaries. They took readily to instruction. They became attached to the priests, who treated them with unalterable kindness. No sooner, however, did they begin to show good dispositions than they were spoiled by the example, and often by the counsel of the elders. Vice was so rampant that it was hopeless to protect the young from its contamination. Accordingly the missionaries concluded that the only remedy was to do what the Franciscans already had attempted when they opened a seminary for the young Indians at Quebec. Daniel was a favorite with mothers and children. There is a pleasant story of his quieting a little child, crying in its mother's arms by having it make the sign of the Cross. He and Davost were promised several children for the new seminary, a dozen at least, but when the day came for departure maternal instinct revolted against parting from the little ones and they had to go down to Quebec with three only. They were the foundation stones. The hope of the missionaries was to remove a number of the young people from the contagious surroundings of their village, bring them up unspoiled, establish a Christian Indian settlement and gradually, no matter how slowly, establish a new civilization among the Indians themselves, which would attract even those who were habituated to corrupt living. This seminary became the apple of their eyes. Extraordinary things are narrated in the "Relations" about the simplicity and innocence of the young boys and of the constancy of many of them afterwards. Similar results on a larger scale were obtained at the seminary of the Ursulines for young girls. Indeed the virtue developed in these schools often mounted to heroism. Le Jeune describes this boys' seminary at length in the "Relation" of 1637.[47] Daniel was teacher, nurse and playmate with the children. They looked upon him as their father, and very touching are the evidences of their devotion to him.

CHAPTER EIGHT
Brébeuf's Ideal Missionary

BRÉBEUF was alone again after the departure of his companions. He knew it would not be for long. Other harvesters were soon to come into the field. Indeed, it was a matter of constant solicitude among the missionaries to have assistants, and in due time successors, who would come fully aware of what was ahead of them, and yet fully prepared not only to meet every privation and hardship, but to labor and to encounter danger of every sort in order to make the natives Christians. This no doubt was in Brébeuf's mind when he wrote his famous instruction for those who were to come to the Huron mission. It sets forth so plainly the trials of a missionary's life, and it appeals so eloquently for volunteers, not because of novelty, or of adventure or of consoling ministerial occupation and results, but solely because of the life of heroic devotion to Christ, that it is well worth giving here as a revelation of the spirit of the apostle himself and of those who would come with their eyes wide open to the prospect before them. Such souls could evidently be satisfied with nothing short of heroism. It is contained in the "Relation" of 1636. How it reminds one of St. Francis Xavier! There is a genius, and there is also a race also, of sanctity.

"When you reach the Hurons, you will indeed find hearts full of charity; we shall receive you with open arms as an angel of paradise, we shall have all the inclination in the world to do you good; but we are so situated that we can do very little. We shall receive you in a hut, so mean that I have scarcely found in France one wretched enough to compare it with; that is how you will be lodged. Harassed and fatigued as you will be, we shall be able to give you nothing but a poor mat, or at most a skin, to serve you as a bed; and, besides, you will arrive at a season when miserable little insects that we call here *taouhac*, and, in good French, *pulces* [fleas], will keep you awake almost all night, for in these countries they are incomparably more troublesome than in France; the dust of the cabin nourishes them, the savages bring them to us, we get them in their houses; and this petty martyrdom, not to speak of mosquitoes, sandflies, and other like vermin, lasts usually not less than three or four months of the summer.

"Instead of being a great master and great theologian as in France, you must reckon on being here a humble scholar, and then, good God! with what masters! — women, little children, and all the savages — and exposed to their laughter. The Huron language will be your Saint Thomas and your Aristotle; and clever man as you are, and speaking glibly among learned and capable persons, you must make up your mind to be for a long

time mute among the barbarians. You will have
accomplished much, if, at the end of a considerable
time, you begin to stammer a little.

"And then how do you think you would pass
the winter with us? After having heard all that
must be endured in wintering among the Mon-
tagnets savages, I may say that that is almost the
life we lead here among the Hurons. I say it
without exaggeration, and five and six months of
winter are spent in almost continual discomforts,—
excessive cold, smoke, and the annoyance of the
savages; we have a cabin built of simple bark, but
so well jointed that we have to send some one outside to learn what kind of weather it is; the smoke
is very often so thick, so annoying, and so obstinate
that, for five or six days at a time, if you are not
entirely proof against it, it is all you can do to
make out a few lines in your Breviary. Besides,
from morning until evening our fireplace is almost
always surrounded by savages,— above all, they
seldom fail to be there at mealtimes. If you
happen to have anything more than usual, let it
be ever so little, you must reckon on most of these
gentlemen as your guests; if you do not share
with them, you will be considered mean. As
regards the food, it is not so bad, although we
usually content ourselves with a little corn, or a
morsel of dry smoked fish, or some fruits, of which
I shall speak further on.

"For the rest, thus far we have had only roses;

henceforth, as we have Christians in almost every village, we must count upon making rounds through them at all seasons of the year, and of remaining there, according to necessity, for two or three whole weeks, amid annoyances that cannot be described. Add to all this, that our lives depend upon a single thread; and if, wherever we are in the world, we are to expect death every hour, and to be prepared for it, this is particularly the case here. For not to mention that your cabin is only, as it were, chaff, and that it might be burned at any moment, despite all your care to prevent accidents, the malice of the savages gives especial cause for almost perpetual fear; a malcontent may burn you down, or cleave your head open in some lonely spot. And then you are responsible for the sterility or fecundity of the earth, under penalty of your life; you are the cause of droughts; if you cannot make rain, they speak of nothing less than making away with you. I have only to mention, in addition, the danger there is from our enemies; it is enough to say that, on the thirteenth of this month of June, they killed twelve of our Hurons near the village of Contarrea, which is only a day's journey from us; that a short time before, at four leagues from our village, some Iroquois were discovered in the fields in ambuscade, only waiting to strike a blow at the expense of the life of some passer-by. This nation is very timid,— they take no precautions against surprise, they are not careful to prepare arms or to inclose their villages with palisades; their usual recourse, especially when the enemy is powerful, is flight. Amid these alarms, which affect the whole country, I leave you to imagine if we have any grounds for a feeling of safety.

"After all, if we had here the exterior attractions of piety, as they exist in France, all this might pass. In France the great multitude and the good example of Christians, the solemnity of the feasts, the majesty of the churches so magnificently adorned, preach piety to you; and in the houses of our Order the fervor of our brethren, their modesty, and all the noble virtues which shine forth in all their actions, are so many powerful voices which cry to you without ceasing, 'Behold, and do likewise'. You have the consolation of celebrating every day the holy Mass; in a word, you are almost beyond the danger of falling,—at least, the falls are insignificant, and you have help immediately at hand. Here we have nothing, it seems, which incites towards good; we are among peoples who are astonished when you speak to them of God, and who often have only horrible blasphemies in their mouths. Often you are compelled to deprive yourself of the Holy Sacrifice of the Mass; and, when you have the opportunity to say it, a little corner of your cabin will serve you for a chapel, which the smoke, the snow, or the rain hinders you from ornamenting and embellishing, even if you had the means. I pass over the small chance of seclusion there is among barbarians, who scarcely ever leave you, who hardly know what it is to speak in a low tone. Especially I would not dare to speak of the danger there is of ruining oneself among their impurities, in the case of any one whose heart is not sufficiently full of God to firmly resist this poison. But enough of this; the rest can only be known by experience.

" 'But is that all?' some one will exclaim. 'Do you think by your arguments to throw water on the fire that consumes me, and lessen ever so little the zeal I have for the conversion of these peoples? I declare that these things have served only to confirm me the more in my vocation; that I feel myself more carried away than ever by my affection for New France, and that I bear a holy jealousy towards those who are already enduring all these sufferings; all these labors seem to me nothing, in comparison with what I am willing to endure for God; if I knew a place under heaven where there was yet more to be suffered, I would go there.' Ah! whoever you are to whom God gives these sentiments and this light, come, come, my dear Brother, it is workmen such as you that we ask for here; it is to souls like yours that God has appointed the conquest of so many other souls whom the Devil holds yet in his power; apprehend no difficulties,— there will be none for you, since it is your whole consolation to see yourself crucified with the Son of God; silence will be sweet to you, since you have learned to commune with God, and to converse in the heavens with saints and angels; the victuals would be very insipid if the gall endured by Our Lord did not render them sweeter and more savory to you than the most delicious viands of the world. What a satisfaction to pass these rapids, and to climb these rocks, to him who has before his eyes that loving Savior, harassed by His tormentors and ascending Calvary laden with His Cross; the discomfort of the canoe is very easy to bear, to him who considers the Crucified One. What a consolation! — for I must use such terms, as otherwise I could not give you pleasure — what a consolation, then, to see oneself even abandoned on the road by the savages, languishing with sickness, or even dying with hunger in the woods, and of being able to say to God, 'My God, it is to do Your Holy Will that I am reduced to the state in which You see me,'— considering above all that God-Man who expires upon the Cross and cries to His Father, 'My God! My God! Oh, why hast Thou abandoned me?' If God among all these hardships preserve you in health, no doubt you will arrive pleasantly in the Huron country with these holy thoughts. 'Favorably sails he whom God's grace urgeth on'.

"And now, as regards a place of abode, food, and beds,— shall I dare to say to a heart so generous, and that mocks at all that of which I have already spoken, that truly, even though we have hardly more of those necessities than the savages have, still, I know not how, the Divine Goodness renders every difficult thing easy; and all and every one of us find everything almost as comfortable as life is in France. The sleep we get lying on our mats seems to us as sweet as if we were in a good bed; the food of the country does not disgust us, although there is scarcely any other seasoning than that which God has put into it; and, notwithstanding the cold of a winter six months long, passed in the shelter of a bark cabin open to the daylight, we have still to experience its evil effects; no one complains of his head or his stomach; we do not know what diarrhoea, colds, or catarrh are. This leads me to say that delicate persons do not know, in France, how to protect themselves from the cold; those rooms so well carpeted, those doors so well fitted, and those windows closed with so much care, serve only to make its effects more keenly felt; it is an enemy from whom one wins almost more by holding out one's hands to him than by waging a cruel war upon him. As to our food, I shall say this further, that God has shown His Providence very clearly to our eyes; we have obtained in eight days our provision of corn for a whole year, without making a single step beyond our cabin. They have brought us dried fish in such quantities that we are constrained to refuse some of it, and to say that we have sufficient; you might say that God, seeing we are here only for His service, in order that all

our work may be for Him, wishes to act Himself
as our provider. This same Goodness takes care
to give us from time to time a change of provisions
in the shape of fresh fish. We live on the shore of
a great lake, which affords as good fish as I have
ever seen or eaten in France; true, as I have said,
we do not ordinarily procure them, and still less
do we get meat, which is even more rarely seen here.
Fruits even, according to the season, provided the
year be somewhat favorable, are not lacking to us;
strawberries, raspberries, and blackberries are to be
found in almost incredible quantities. We gather
plenty of grapes, which are fairly good; the
squashes last sometimes four and five months, and
are so abundant that they are to be had almost
for nothing, and so good that, on being cooked in
the ashes, they are eaten as apples are in France.
Consequently, to tell the truth, as regards provisions, the change from France is not very great;
the only grain of the country is a sufficient nourish-
ment, when one is somewhat accustomed to it. The
savages prepare it in more than twenty ways and
yet employ only fire and water; it is true that
the best sauce is that which it carries with it.

"As for the dangers of the soul, to speak frankly,
there are none for him who brings to the country
of the Hurons the fear and love of God; on the
contrary, I find unparalleled advantages for acquir-
ing perfection. Is it not a great deal to have, in
one's food, clothing, and sleep, no other attraction

than bare necessity? Is it not a glorious opportunity to unite oneself with God, when there is no
creature whatsoever that gives you reason to spend
your affection upon it? When the exercises you
practice constrain you without force to inward
meditation? Besides your spiritual exercises, you
have no other employment than the study of the
language, and conversation with the savages. Ah!
how much pleasure there is for a heart devoted to
God to make itself the little scholar of a savage
and of a little child, thereby to gain them for God,
and to render them disciples of Our Lord! How
willingly and liberally God communicates Himself
to a soul which practises from love to Him these
heroic acts of humility! The words he learns are
so many treasures he amasses, so many spoils he
carries off from the common enemy of the human
race; so that he has reason to say a hundred times
a day, 'I will rejoice in thy words as one that hath
found great spoil'. Viewed in this light, the
visits of the savages, however frequent, cannot be
annoying to him. God teaches him the beautiful
lesson He taught formerly to Saint Catherine of
Sienna, to make of his heart a room or temple for
Him, where he will never fail to find Him, as often
as he withdraws into it; that, if he encounters
savages there, they do not interfere with his prayers,
they serve only to make them more fervent; from
this he takes occasion to present these poor wretches

to this Sovereign Goodness, and to entreat Him warmly for their conversion.

"Certainly we have not here that exterior solemnity which awakens and sustains devotion. Only what is essential to our religion is visible, the Holy Sacrament of the Altar, to the marvels of which we must open the eyes of our faith without being aided by any sensible mark of its grandeur, any more than the Magi were in the stable. But it seems that God, supplying what we lack,— and as a recompense of grace that he has given us in transporting it, so to speak, beyond so many seas, and in finding a place for it in these poor cabins,— wishes to crown us with the same blessings, in the midst of these infidel peoples, with which he is accustomed to favor persecuted Catholics in the countries of heretics. These good people scarcely ever see either church or altar; but the little they see is worth double what they would see in full liberty. What consolation would there be, in your opinion, in prostrating ourselves at times before a cross in the midst of this barbarism! to turn our eyes toward, and to enter, in the midst of our petty domestic duties, even into the room which the Son of God has been pleased to take in our little dwelling! Is it not to be in paradise day and night, that we are not separated from this Well-Beloved of the Nations except by some bark or the branch of a tree? 'Behold he stands at our window. I sat under his shadow whom I desired'.

See what we have within. If we go outside our
cabin, heaven is open to us; and those great
buildings which lift their heads to the clouds, in
large cities, do not conceal it from our view; so
that we can say our prayers in full liberty before
the noble oratory that Saint Francis Xavier loved
better than any other. If the question is of the
fundamental virtues, I will glory not in myself, but
in the share which has fallen to me; or, if I must,
acknowledge it humbly beside the cross which Our
Lord in his grace gives us to bear after him. Certain
it is that this country, or our work here, is much
more fitted to feed the soul with the fruits of
heaven than with the fruits of earth. I may be
deceiving myself, but I imagine that here is a grand
means of increasing the soul in faith, in hope, and
in charity. Should we scatter the seeds of the Faith
without ourselves profiting by them? Could we
put our confidence anywhere but in God in a region
where, as far as man is concerned, everything is
lacking to us? Could we wish a nobler opportunity
to exercise charity than amid the roughness and
discomfort of a New World, where no human art
or industry has yet provided any conveniences? and
to live here that we may bring back to God men
who are so unlike men that we must live in daily
expectation of dying by their hand, should the
fancy take them, should a dream suggest it to them,
or should we fail to open or close the heavens to
them at discretion, giving them rain or fine weather

at command. Do they not make us responsible for the state of the weather? And if God does not inspire us, or if we cannot work miracles by faith, are we not continually in danger, as they have threatened us, of seeing them fall upon those who have done no wrong? Indeed, if He who is the Truth itself had not declared that there is no greater love than to lay down one's life, verily and once for all, for one's friends, I should conceive it a thing equally noble, or even more so, to do what the Apostle said to the Corinthians, 'Daily I die, I protest by your glory, brethren, whom I have in Christ Jesus Our Lord', than to drag out a life full of misery, amid the frequent and ordinary dangers of an unforeseen death, which those whom you hope to save will procure for you. I call to mind occasionally when Saint Francis Xavier once wrote to Father Simon, and wish that it may please God to so act that at least the same thing may be said or written one day even of us, although we may not be worthy of it. Here are the words: 'The best of news comes from Molucca, that John Beira and his companions are constantly in trial and in danger of life, with much progress for the Christian Religion'.

CHAPTER NINE

Arrival of Jogues and Garnier

A. D. 1636–1640

Recruits—Voyage overseas—A martyr and a Mother—
Brébeuf again isolated—Four auxiliaries—Arrival of Jogues—
Illness in tribe and Mission—A missionary's daily routine—An
Indian's cabin—Mission at Ossossané—Vacation and summer
school.

BEFORE Brébeuf's letter reached France recruits were already on the way who would soon be with him in Huronia. His dream was to come true. No doubt in that isolation and solitude, he spent long hours imagining and longing and praying for the realization of his soul's desire. The Jesuits in France had engaged to supply missionaries, and their engagement was like that of a nation pledging troops for war. The number eager to enlist in this case made it difficult for superiors to name who would be first to venture overseas. Early in 1636 they chose five among them, Jogues who was to be apostle to a new Indian nation, and martyr also, along with Garnier, another of the choice company. The others were Adam, Ragueneau and Chastellain, with a brother Cauvet. They came with the new Governor Montmagny in a fleet of eight vessels, leaving Dieppe on April 8th, arriving in Chaleurs Bay June 1st, Jogues moving up to Quebec July 2nd. Two months was

the usual time for the voyage. It often took four.
Lalemant spent three months on the way. Cartier
made his first trip in a ship of sixty tons, in twenty
days. It was always tedious, often stormy and very
dangerous. The missionaries were distributed
among the vessels. Jogues and Garnier were on
the same ship. The crew behaved far better than
the lot that went with Poutrincourt. One of them,
however, was a notorious backslider, and to him the
angelic Garnier paid every attention. Before many
days this man yielded to the good priest's influence
and sought reconciliation with his Church.
Garnier's interest in prison inmates when a student
in Paris, led him to be concerned about difficult
cases. This will appear frequently in his dealings
with the Indians.

Our first intimate knowledge of Jogues is derived
from letters to his mother, which were quite frequent. There was one before leaving Dieppe,
another on reaching Quebec, and a third within
another month before starting for the Huron country. To him she was, after the word of the Com-
mandment, Honored Mother, as he addressed her.
More than ever the title befits her now. The
first of these messages was:

". . . Endeavor also, if you please, to contribute something by your prayers to the safety of
our voyage, and chiefly by a generous resignation
of your will to that of God, conforming your desires
to those of the Divine goodness, which can be only

most holy and honorable for us, since they spring from the heart of a Father full of love for our welfare.

"I hope, as I said on another occasion, that if you take this little affliction in a proper spirit, it will be most pleasing to God, for whose sake it would become you to give not one son only, but all the others, nay, life itself, if it were necessary. Men for a little gain cross the seas, enduring, at least, as much as we; and shall we not, for God's love, do what men do for earthly interests?

"Good-by, dear mother. I thank you for all the affection which you have ever shown me, and above all at our last meeting. May God unite us in His holy paradise, if we do not see each other again on earth!

"Present my most humble recommendations to my brothers and sisters, to whose prayers, as to yours, I commend myself in heart and love.

"Your most humble son and obedient servant in Our Lord,

ISAAC JOGUES.

DIEPPE, April 6, 1636."[49]

He wrote to her after arriving at Quebec:

"I do not know what it is to enter paradise; but this I know, that it is difficult to experience in this world a joy more excessive and more overflowing than that I felt on my setting foot in New France, and celebrating my first Mass here on the day of the Visitation. I assure you it was indeed a day of the visitation of the goodness of God and Our Lady. I felt as if it were a Christmas day for me, and that I was to be born again to a new life, and a life in God."[50]

Before leaving for the Huron mission he wrote still another letter on August 20th, as follows:

". . . My health has been so good, thank God, at sea and on land that it has been a matter of wonder to all, it being very unusual for any one to make such a long voyage without suffering a little from sea-sickness or nausea. The vestments and chapel service have been a great comfort to me, as I have offered the holy sacrifice of Mass every day the weather was favorable — a happiness I should have been deprived of, had not our family provided me with them. It was a great consolation to me, and one which our Fathers did not enjoy the preceding years. Officers and crew have profited by it; as but for that the eighty persons on board could not have been present at the Holy Sacrifice for two months, whilst, owing to the faculties I enjoyed, they all confessed and received communion at Whitsunday, Ascension, and Corpus Christi. God will reward you and Madam Houdelin for the good you have enabled me to do.

"You shall have letters of mine every year, and I shall expect yours. It will ever be a consolation for me to hear from you and our family, as I have no hope of seeing you in our lifetime. May God in His goodness unite us both in His holy abode to praise Him for all eternity!"[51]

It was not intended at first that Jogues should go immediately to the Hurons. For a time Brébeuf was there alone. He went through all the excitement of a threatened Iroquois invasion, and he had to witness the revolting scene of an Iroquois tortured unto death. He was powerless to prevent this, but as he had baptized the captive shortly before his ordeal, he was determined to stand by, console and encourage him through such hellish treatment. It was then he witnessed an exhibition of Indian character which was new to him. Their mockery of the victim was fiendish. The more they burned his flesh and crushed his bones, the more they flattered and even coddled him. It was an all-night tragedy. Brebéuf was witnessing what he himself would afterwards suffer.

Le Mercier and Pijart had gone up while Daniel and Davost were on their way down; Garnier and Chastellain went there directly, meeting Daniel on the way. Five would be enough for the time being. Providence had other designs. About August 20th, Daniel's canoe came into Three Rivers with his young charges, and Jogues was there to witness his arrival.

"Father Daniel was in this first company, Father Davost in the rear guard, which did not yet appear; and we even began to doubt whether the island savages had not made them return. At the sight of Father Daniel, our hearts melted; his face was gay and happy, but greatly emaciated; he was bare-footed, had a paddle in his hand, and was clad in a wretched cassock, his Breviary suspended to his neck, his shirt rotting on his back. He saluted our captains and our French people; then we embraced him, and, having led him to our little room, after having blessed and adored Our Lord, he related to us in what condition was the cause of Christianity among the Hurons, delivering to me the letters and the Relation sent from that country, which constrained us to sing a *Te Deum*, as a thanksgiving for the blessings that God was pouring out upon this new Church. I shall not speak of the difficulties of his voyage, all that has been already told; it was enough for him that he baptized a poor wretch they were leading to his death, to sweeten all his trials."[52]

The Indians begged that a priest should accompany them homeward, and Jogues was selected for this errand. They left on St. Bartholomew's Day, August 24th. At his first opportunity for getting a letter through, June 1st the following year, he wrote to his mother describing the journey with the same detail as Brébeuf in Chapter Four, but more briefly, and with a story in addition about a sick Indian child whom he had to look after, lifting him out of the canoe, carrying him over the portages. Now he is with his Indians and he can speak freely with a mother.

". . . Nothing can equal the satisfaction enjoyed in our hearts while we impart the knowledge of the True God to these heathen. About two hundred and forty have received baptism this year; among them I have baptized some who surely are now in heaven, as they were children one or two years old.

"Can we think the life of man better employed than in this good work? What do I say? Would not all the labors of a thousand men be well rewarded in the conversion of a single soul gained to Jesus Christ? I have always felt a great love for this kind of life, and for a profession so excellent, and so akin to that of the Apostles. Had I to work for this happiness alone, I would exert myself to my utmost to obtain a favor, for which I would fain give a thousand lives.

"Should you receive these lines, I entreat you, by the bonds of the love of Jesus Christ, to give thanks to the Lord for this extraordinary favor He has bestowed upon me — a favor so earnestly wished and craved by many servants of God endowed with qualities far above what I possess."[53]

If, instead, of writing, he had gone home to her, one wonders if she could have greeted him more affectionately than did his fellows at Ihonatiria. As Ragueneau writes in the Relation for that year:

"I made all the preparations for his reception; but oh, what a feast! — a handful of little dried fish, with a sprinkling of flour. I sent for a few

ears of corn, which we roasted for him after the
fashion of the country. But it is true that at heart,
and to hear him, he never enjoyed better cheer.
The happiness felt at these meetings seems to
reflect in some sort the joy of the blessed on their
entrance into heaven, so full of sweetness is it!"[54]

An epidemic was raging in the village and Jogues
was its first victim, among the missionaries.
Garnier, Adam, Ragueneau and Chastellain followed. For a while Jogues lay at death's door.
As a desperate remedy bleeding was resorted to,
and Jogues acted successfully as his own surgeon.
He made a rapid recovery. In October he was
about again. The others came round more slowly.
All, even the convalescing, did what they could to
minister to the afflicted Indians. Even in that time
medical attention to the body was a way of
approach to the soul. The Indians took what relief
was afforded them, but ungratefully blamed the
Fathers for having brought on their illness. The
village sorcerer Tonneraouanont had offered to cure
the Fathers by his incantations. He resented their
declining. When he saw them grow well without
his aid, he was convinced that they were greater
sorcerers than himself. It was not difficult for him
and others like him to spread the impression that
by evil arts the priests had brought this affliction
on the village. Fortunately on this occasion the
missionaries could prove that the village was the

source of the contagion, but they could not remove every lurking suspicion, as the sequel will show.

The new arrivals were busy with the language. In Brébeuf they had an excellent master and they all made quick progress. They made regular visits to the cabins, following as best they could the daily order detailed in a letter of François du Peron three years later:

"The importunity of the savages,— who are continually about us in our cabin, and who sometimes break down a door, throw stones at our cabin, and wound our people,— this importunity, I say, does not prevent our observance of our hours, as well regulated as in one of our colleges in France. At four o'clock the rising-bell rings; then follows the orison, at the end of which the Masses begin and continue until eight o'clock; during this period each one keeps silent, reads his spiritual book, and says his lesser hours. At eight o'clock, the door is left open to the savages, until four in the evening; it is permitted to talk with the savages at this time, as much to instruct them as to learn their language. In this time, also, our Fathers visit the cabins of the town, to baptize the sick and to instruct the well; as for me, my employment is the study of the language, watching the cabin, helping the Christians and catechumens pray to God, and keeping school for their children from noon until two o'clock, when the bell rings for examination of conscience. Then follows the dinner, during which is read some

chapter from the Bible; and at supper Reverend
Father du Barry's Philagie of Jesus is read; the
Benedicite and grace is said in Huron, on account
of the savages who are present. We dine around
the fire, seated on a log, with our plates on the
ground. At noon I open the school for the children
who happen to be there up to two o'clock; sometimes I only have one, two, or three pupils. On
Sundays, Tuesdays, and Thursdays, school closes at
one o'clock, when instruction is given to the most
prominent people of the village, whether Christians
or not; on Thursdays, to Christians and catechumens
only; on Sunday morning, to Christians only. During the parochial Mass, the sermon is preached;
before the Mass, the water is blessed while they are
singing; and at the offertory the bread, which the
savages present in turn, is blessed. On great holy
days, High Mass is celebrated. After dinner on Sundays, at one o'clock, vespers are sung; then follows
the instruction of Christians and catechumens;
at five o'clock complines are sung, and on Saturday
evening the *Salve*, with the litanies of the Virgin.
On this same day, at the close of school, a short
catechetical instruction is given to the children;
and once a month a public catechism is given to
the whole village besides the daily instruction given
them in their cabins. At four o'clock in the
evening, the savages who are not Christians are sent
away, and we quietly say, all together, our matins
and lauds, at the end of which we hold mutual

consultation for three-quarters of an hour about the advancement of and the hindrances to the Faith in these countries; afterwards we confer together about the language until supper, which is at half-past six; at eight o'clock, the litanies, examination of conscience, and then we retire to sleep."[55]

This is what a visit to the cabins meant:

"If you go to visit them in their cabins,—and you must go there oftener than once a day, if you would perform your duty as you ought,— you will find there a miniature picture of hell,— seeing nothing, ordinarily, but fire and smoke, and on every side naked bodies, black and half roasted, mingled pell-mell with the dogs, which are held as dear as the children of the house, and share the beds, plates, and food of their masters. Everything is in a cloud of dust, and, if you go within, you will not reach the end of the cabin before you are completely befouled with soot, filth, and dirt."[56]

A pleasanter picture is that of the missionary's mode of spending his vacation, and of his summer school:

"Summer here is a very inconvenient season for instructing the savages. Their trading expeditions and the farms take every one away, men, women, and children — almost no one remains in the villages. I will tell you how we spent last summer.

"In the first place, we all came together for the spiritual exercises, as is the custom of our Society. We had the more need of these exercises,

as the high duties we are called upon to perform
need more union with God, and because we are
compelled to live in a continual bustle. For this
reason we often acknowledge that those who come
here should bring a good reserve fund of virtue, if
they wish here to gather the fruits thereof. After
our exercises we made a confused memorandum of
the words we had learned since our arrival, and
then we outlined a dictionary of the Huron language
which will be very profitable. In it will be seen
the various meanings; one will easily recognize in
it, when the words are grouped, their differences,
which consist sometimes in only a single letter, or
even in an accent. Finally we busied ourselves
in revising, or rather in arranging, a grammar. I
fear we shall often have to make similar revisions;
for every day we discover new secrets in this science,
which for the present hinders us from sending anything to be printed. We know now, thank God,
sufficient to understand and to be understood, but
not yet to publish. It is indeed an exceedingly
laborious task to endeavor to understand in all
points a foreign tongue, very abundant, and as
different from our European languages as heaven
is from earth,— and that without master or books.
I say no more about it here, as I shall write a
chapter about it, further on. We all work at it
diligently; it is one of our most common occupations. There is not one of us who does not already
talk a jargon, and make himself understood, the

newly-arrived Fathers as well as the others. I trust that Father Mercier, in particular, will soon be master of it."[57]

Brébeuf will write to the General of his Order in May, 1637:

". . . We are gladly heard, we have baptized more than two hundred this year, and there is hardly a village that has not invited us to go to it. Besides, the result of this pestilence and of these reports has been to make us better known to this people; and at last it is understood, from our actions and from our truths [of religion], that we have not come hither to buy skins or carry on any traffic, but solely to teach them and win them to Christ, and to procure for them their souls' health, and finally everlasting and immortal life. Furthermore, since some families, although not yet baptized, rested all their hope in the Lord, and therefore almost alone remained safe and unharmed, it has resulted that they believe, and eagerly ask for baptism, which, as we hope, they will receive, when they shall have been sufficiently proved. We have seen, too, no uncertain signs of present grace in many whom we have purified through baptism; and already many, both old and young, have, as we believe, soared away to heaven, blessed intercessors before God for their friends. Finally, we have come to hope that — this pestilence, which still rages, once abated in due season, and the minds of men restored to that tranquillity necessary to the hearing and understanding of the truths of the Faith — very many will be converted."[58]

Later when the contagion was at an end, in 1639 Jogues wrote to his brother:

"During the epidemic the Fathers baptized more than one thousand two hundred persons. Even in the village where they were the most exposed to the perversity of the people, there were always some anxious to follow the instructions of our Fathers; about one hundred have been regenerated in the waters of baptism, amongst them twenty-two little children."[59]

CHAPTER TEN
Brébeuf's Ideal Realized
A. D. 1639

Hostility to missionaries—Imported prejudices—Dream and transport—Baptism of first adult in health—Council decides on death of missionaries—A marvellous document—A new Mission—An Indian census—Conversions begin

THE plague was so persistent, the chiefs convoked a council at Ossossané to deliberate on measures for eradicating it. Brébeuf and Jogues were present. Brébeuf began with prayer, distributed tobacco for the calumets, and backed with presents his proposal that the Indians give up superstitious practices, implore God's mercy and adopt the Faith. The immediate thing to do was to erect a chapel. They all seemed to agree. They held their banquet, but their resolution was by no means stable. At Ihonatiria the missionaries had to face a new outbreak of suspicion and prejudice. The hostility to the Jesuits, especially in the Lutheran countries of Europe, followed them into Huronia through the Dutch settlement at Rensselaerswyck, now Albany. The burghers did not mean to incite the Hurons to molest their missionaries. This they proved later by their persistent efforts to obtain the release of Jogues from his Mohawk captors, and their pride in aiding his escape. They meant to warn them against accepting what they preached, giving as a reason that these men had brought on a blight in every country that tolerated them. Some of the Indians, who disliked the opposition of the missionaries to their superstitions, interpreted this to mean that the Jesuits had been the cause of their misfortunes. Everything they had and everything they did became suspect, their crucifix, their Breviary, clock, magnetic needle, the Sign of the Cross, kneeling to pray, writing a letter. Sorcerers themselves, the Indians adjudged everyone else the same. The situation became so trying that Jerome Lalemant wrote in the "Relation" for 1639:

". . . I begin to doubt whether any other martyrdom is requisite for the end for which we labor; and I have not the least doubt that many would be found who would rather feel at once the keen edge of a hatchet on their head, than endure for years a life such as we have to live here every day."[60]

Dreams go by contraries. With all this agitation against them the missionaries maintained their usual calmness. Jogues' mind apparently was not disturbed by it. Endeavoring to overcome sleep one afternoon when in the chapel, he gave way for a moment, and dreamed that he was singing Vespers. The verse, "Give ear, O Lord, unto my prayer", of the Fifth Psalm was sung, and then as he tells us:

"When the verse was ended, I seemed to be no longer in our cabin, but in a place I knew not, when all at once I heard verses sung (I forget which) which had reference to the happiness of the Saints, and the delights they enjoy in the kingdom of heaven. The chanting was so beautiful, and the melody of voices and instruments so harmonious, that I have no recollection of ever having heard the like, and it even seems to me that the most perfect concerts are nothing compared to it. To compare such harmony with that of earth would be insulting.

"Meanwhile this most admirable concert of the angels excited in my heart a love of God so great, so ardent, so burning, that, unable to bear such an overflowing of sweetness, my poor heart seemed to melt and dilate under this inexplicable wealth of Divine love. I experienced this feeling especially as they sang the verse I so well remember, 'We will go into His tabernacle, we will adore in the place where His feet stood'.[61]

This lasted but a moment. It suggests strongly that his thoughts and aspirations were so far above mundane things that neither persecution nor actual torture could affect him even when dreaming.

Life at Ihonatiria became impossible for the missionaries. Their work was hampered. The people were decimated by the epidemic. They were urged to settle in Ossossané (near Point Varwood on Nottawasaga Bay), and also at Teanaustayé, inland (near Hillsdale, in Medonté township), known as St. Joseph II. A chapel was built for them at the former place, eighty feet in length, with real boards and doors, and it was soon the scene of the baptism of Tsiouendaentaha, the first adult in good health admitted to baptism in that mission, after three years' labor of an average of five men! There was humor as well as fitness in the name given him, Peter, since he was to be the corner-stone of Christianity in that remote region. The ceremony was solemn. The Indians, who loved ceremonial, flocked to it. The enemies of the missionaries made it an occasion of renewed hostility. The Fathers were unmoved. Brébeuf had the sachems call an assembly, appeared before it, and convinced them, apparently at least, that they were wrong in attributing sorcery to the priests. With quiet restored for a time, the work of the mission prospered.

Like all untutored minds, the Indian's was one of fixed ideas. Once seized with a belief, right or wrong, it was useless to argue with him. Early in August another council was called, ostensibly to consider tribal affairs, but in reality to determine the fate of the Jesuits. Twenty-eight villages were represented. Brébeuf was present. The first day was given to indifferent matters; on the second the session was in the evening, lasting until midnight. It was plain to Brébeuf that he and his companions were doomed. He was on trial. They abused and accused him. He defended himself fearlessly. Their decision was deferred until the return of their tribesmen from Quebec. An attempt was made to burn the mission cabin; the young men of the tribe harassed the Fathers where-ever they met them. On October 4th, they were summoned to meet the elders of the tribe and informed that they should die. Brébouf went about among the captains to obtain a stay of pro-ceedings, but to no purpose. It was at this juncture he indited a statement as heroic as any contained in the Acts of the Martyrs. Everyone at the mis-sion signed it. Those who were absent made known their assent.

"My Reverend Father,
The Peace of Christ.

"We are, perhaps, upon the point of shedding our blood and of sacrificing our lives to the service of our good Master, Jesus Christ. It seems that His goodness consents to accept this sacrifice from me for the expiation of my great and innumerable sins, and to crown from this time on, the past services and the great and ardent desires of all our Fathers who are here.

"What makes me think that this will not hap-pen is, on the one hand, the excess of my past wickedness, which renders me utterly unworthy of so signal a favor; and, on the other, that I do not believe His goodness will permit His workmen to be put to death, since through His grace there are still some good souls who eagerly receive the seed of the Gospel, notwithstanding the evil speech and persecutions of all men against us. And yet I fear that Divine justice, seeing the obstinacy of the majority of these barbarians in their follies, may very justly permit them to come and take away the life of the body from those who with all their hearts desire and procure the life of their souls.

"Be this as it may, I will tell you that all our Fathers await the outcome of this affair with great calmness and contentment of mind. And, for myself, I can say to your reverence with all sincerity that I have not yet had the least apprehension of death for such a cause. But we are all sorry for this—that these poor barbarians, through their own malice, are closing the door to the Gospel and to grace. Whatever conclusion they reach, and whatever treatment they give us, we will try, by the grace of Our Lord, to endure it patiently for His service. It is a singular favor that His goodness extends to us, to make us endure something for His sake. It is now that we consider ourselves truly to belong to His Society. May He be forever blessed for having appointed us to this country, among many others better than we, to aid Him in bearing His Cross. In all things, may His holy will be done! If He will that at this hour we should die, oh, fortunate hour for us! If He will to reserve us for other labors, may He be blessed! If you hear that God has crowned our insignificant labors, or rather our desires, bless Him; for it is for

Him that we desire to live and to die, and it is He who gives us grace therefor. For the rest, if any survive, I have given orders as to all they are to do. I have deemed it advisable for our Fathers and our domestics to withdraw to the houses of those whom they regard as their best friends; I have charged them to carry to the house of Pierre, our first Christian, all that belongs to the sacristy,— above all, to be especially careful to put our dictionary, and all that we have of the language, in a place of safety. As for myself, if God grant me the grace to go to heaven, I will pray Him for them, for the poor Hurons, and I will not forget your reverence.

"And finally, we supplicate your reverence and all our Fathers not to forget us in your holy Sacrifices and prayers, to the end that, in life after death, He may grant us mercy. We are all, in life and in eternity,

> Your Reverence's
>> *Very humble and very affectionate*
>> *servants in Our Lord,*
>>> Jean de Brébeuf.
>>> François Joseph le Mercier.
>>> Pierre Chastellain.
>>> Charles Garnier.
>>> Paul Ragueneau.

In the Residence of la Conception
at Ossossané, this 28th of October.

"I have left Fathers Pierre Pijart and Isaac Jogues in the Residence of Saint Joseph, with the same sentiments."[62]

The Dictionary was the one precious possession of the missionaries. In it was the fruit of years of labor of many men. In it too was hope for the future, as it would facilitate the work of those who would still come to preach Christ to this people. After that Brébeuf does the redoubtable thing which meant in Indian custom that all was ready for the execution. He invited them to his farewell feast, his *Atsataion*, the banquet they themselves gave when they were near death. They filled the cabin. He harangued them not about himself but about life after death. They departed gloomy and irresolute. The missionaries were left in peace. Brébeuf was adopted by the tribe and made a captain. Occasional attacks were made on some of the missionaries, on du Peron, Le Mercier, Chaumont and Ragueneau, but they were the frenzy of individuals, not of the tribe nor of its leaders.

In 1638, Mass was said in the cabin of Stephen Totiri at Teanaustayé, and there a new mission was established, with Brébeuf in charge. Jogues was at that post. Stephen was to be later his companion in captivity. The report for the first year of that mission alone mentioned baptisms of forty-eight children and seventy-two adults. Soon there were nine missionaries in the two villages, among them Le Moyne, who was to be the apostle of the

Onondagas and follow Jogues in his work among
the Mohawks. A census was taken. It was not a
difficult matter. An Indian village was a collection
of cabins, not all as well constructed as that of the
missionaries, but somewhat like it. These stood in
rows more or less regular, and they were as a rule
surrounded by a fence or palisade for protection
against assault by an enemy. There were thirty-
two villages and about twelve thousand inhabitants. Twenty years before they were forty
thousand, but war, famine and epidemics had
reduced their number. The baptism of Peter had
been followed by other conversions. Le Mercier
reports for the year 1638 more than one hundred
baptisms of adults and children, fifty-six of whom
were living when he wrote. Among these was
Joseph Chihwatenhwa of Ossossané, a man of great
natural goodness, who after baptism practised virtue to an extraordinary degree. If the harvest was
slow in ripening, the yield was not disappointing.
Le Jeune gives this account of Joseph's solid Christianity:

". . . I will content myself with saying what
cannot often enough be said: 1. That he has an
extreme horror of sin, hardly ever speaking to us
that he does not propose some question of conscience, his being very sensitive. 2. That he
preaches Jesus Christ boldly and on all occasions,
both by example and by words; he made this con-
spicuous in the councils which I have mentioned

above. He is especially admirable in the continual instruction of those in his cabin, inculcating on them at every opportunity the holy commandments of God. 3. That he has special communication with God, begging Him every day, with tears in his eyes, that it may please Him to look with pity upon his poor country,—so that it is one of our greatest consolations to be near him when he is offering his prayers, above all, his thanksgiving after the Communion. 4. Before and after the instructions that are given him, it is a pleasure to see him on his knees asking grace of the Divine Spirit; even going so far as to force himself to learn to write, this winter, that he may remember and repeat what was said to him; but, above all, to indicate more clearly, he said, the number of his sins. 5. He makes habitual an incredible purity of conscience, often throwing himself at our feet to confess, exhibiting scruples at the least thing. 6. He will sometimes continue in prayer for three-quarters of an hour, all the time on his knees, which is a very difficult position for a savage. 7. Finally, it is wonderful how much strength God gives him to combat at every turn the great difficulties that the Devil continues to raise for him through the people of his nation,—some by inviting him to their infamous and superstitious feasts, others by openly ridiculing him. He said to us one day with his usual simplicity, 'Yes, my brothers, I am so determined to maintain even unto death the fidelity

I have vowed to my God, that if any one wished to make me return to my former follies, he should sooner take away my life.' In short, his devotion may be summarized as a holy tenderness of heart that God gives him, for the great and loving respect that he shows to the holy Sacrament, for the honor he renders to his guardian angel and his great Patron, and for commending to the holy Virgin his country and the souls of the faithful departed."[63]

Such were the rewards of the missionaries, who would toil for months to win one soul. The souls they won were often not the lost sheep they had gone out to seek, but others who came in their way haphazard, like this one, for instance.

"On our way to a place, we go astray unawares, and find ourselves involved in routes that we were not seeking. We meet two little children who are dying,—prostrate near their mother, who is all in tears; they both receive baptism, and then take flight to heaven. Was it not God who guided us?

"On the eve of All Saints, I am constrained to run alone into two or three cabins, in the midst of a dense forest, where the disease was ruining them. I set foot in a poor little house where I had never entered; I find a young lad in very great danger of dying. I instruct him, and prepare him for holy baptism; his father opposes it, and will not allow me this, unless at the same time I baptize another, who is still in the cradle. I object to that, this smaller one being nowise sick; the father, on

his side, also persists in his refusal, telling me that
he wished that, if his two children died, they should
go in company, either to heaven or to hell. I am
constrained to grant him what he desires, in order
not to lose a soul; I then baptize them both. After
eight days I return; I find them no longer alive; I
am driven from the cabin, and they will hear no
further mention of God. Thus it is that Our Lord
uses even reprobates in order to possess His elect.

"I pass near a cabin where three little children
are dying; I am called, as if I were a great phys-
ician, to declare how much life was left to them.
On going in, I plainly see that they still had
enough left to make them live forever in heaven;
while feeling their pulses, I take my opportunity
secretly, and baptize them; they were awaiting
nothing but that in order to die to all their miseries.
In a word, we are transacting the affairs of God
here: is it a wonder that He takes part in them?"[64]

CHAPTER ELEVEN
More Missions and New Fields
A.D. 1639–1642

A change of policy—A mission centre and more stations—
The missions and greater New France—Motive of the mission-
aries—Not after trade or land—Personnel of the head-quarters
—Individual characteristics—Obedience—Jesuit auxiliaries—
Exploring new fields—Tobacco Indians, Garnier's report—
Jogues and the Ojibways—The Neuters—Brébeuf at Quebec
—Failure and hope of the Mission.

THE year 1639 was marked by a complete
change of policy on the part of the Huron
missionaries. At his earnest solicitation, Brébeuf
had been relieved of his charge of the missions in
August, 1638, and Jerome Lalemant was appointed
in his place. His first move, early the following
year, with the agreement of all the Fathers, was to
establish a head-quarters, or central bureau for the
missions, at a distance from the Indian villages,
with a home to accommodate the priests, their attendants and the Frenchmen, about fifteen in number, who served as soldiers or laborers. The new
location was named Ste-Marie. It was situated
on the Wye River which connected two lakes, on
a peninsula between Midland Bay and Victoria
Harbor, about eight miles from Ossossané, and
twelve from Teanaustayé. The pioneers had
bravely and self-sacrificingly lived with and like
the natives for five years. Experience taught them
that to identify themselves with any one village,

no matter how central, made them less welcome
in the others; that they could not depend on any
group to remain long in the same place; that with
their own cabin as a rendezvous they were not free
to attend to their work. From a central station
they could not only visit at due intervals all the
Huron tribes, but also make occasional excursions
or explorations into the countries of tribes to the
west and south. They built a commodious house
where all the priests could assemble and confer
from time to time; dwellings for their retainers;
a hospital for the sick from the villages and a recep-
tion-place for those who would come for instruction
or for the ceremonies. A fort was erected, the ruins
of which still show the skill of a military engineer;
and finally there was a God's acre for the burial
of all who would die members of the Church.

The new settlement was approved and aided by
the governor at Quebec, and by Richelieu, who saw
in it a station for developing exploration and trade
with the Indians west and south-west. It was really
the beginning of a greater New France. Its origi-
nator, Lalemant, had in view a northern Paraguay
Reduction; its civil promoters looked to it for terri-
torial expansion and commerce. That was the difference in motive between missionary and
mercenary. Very soon the opponents of the former
would fail to see this difference and accuse the
priests of seeking land and fur. Fortunately, those
who had trade primarily in view came to their

defence. The statement they issued is a remarkable one, as Vimont the Jesuit Superior at Quebec gives it in the Relation of 1642:

"Those who believe that the Jesuits go into this end of the world in order to make traffic of skins of dead beasts, account them very rash, and destitute of sense, to go and expose themselves to such horrible dangers, for a benefit so sordid. It seems to me that they have more generous hearts; and that only God and the salvation of souls can make them leave their native land, and the comfort of France, in order to go in quest of fires and torments in the midst of barbarism. Forasmuch, nevertheless, as this error about commerce might slip into the minds of those who are not acquainted with them, it has been judged proper to affix here an authentic attestation, which will show how far they are removed from such thoughts. If they who speak of them with freedom, for want of knowing them, chanced to be with them in that new world, they would certainly change their tone; and, becoming companions in their sufferings and their zeal, they would find themselves united and bound by like affections; and these chains might be eternal, since true love and true charity pass beyond time. Enough; let us conclude with a genuine and impartial testimonial, which may be drawn from the lips of honorable persons, who have stamped it with their names and confirmed it with their signatures.

DECLARATION OF MESSIEURS THE DIRECTORS AND
ASSOCIATES IN THE COMPANY OF NEW FRANCE.

The Directors and Associates in the Company of
New France, called Canada, having learned that
some persons persuade themselves, and circulate the
report, that the Society of the Jesuit Fathers has
part in the shipments, returns, and commercial
transactions which are made in the said country,—
wishing by this device to disparage and destroy
the reputation and value of the great labors which
they undertake in the said country, with pains and
fatigues incredible, and in peril of their lives, for
the service and glory of God, in the conversion of
the savages to the faith of Christianity and the
Catholic, Apostolic, and Roman religion, in which
they have made and are making great progress every
year, whereof the said Society is very intimately
informed,—have believed themselves obliged by
the duty of Christian charity, to undeceive those
who might have this belief, through the declaration
and certification which they make by these presents:
that the said Jesuit Fathers are not associated in
the said Company of New France, directly or indi-
rectly, and have no part in the traffic of merchan-
dise which is carried on by it. In witness whereof
the present declaration has been signed by the said
directors and associates, and sealed with the seal
of the said company, at Paris, in the regular assembly of the same, the first day of December one
thousand six hundred and forty-three. Thus signed:

De la Ferté, Abbé de sainte Magdeleine, Bordier, Margonne, Beruyer, Robineau, Tabouret, Berruyer, Verdier, Fleuriau, Caset, Bourguet, and Clarentin; and sealed with a Seal.

Collated with the original by me, Counsellor, and Secretary of the King, house, and Crown of France.

JOLLY,"[65]

No such statement was needed by those who were acquainted with the actual work of the missionaries. Nor will anyone now repeat the accusation that they were seeking landed properties, seigneuries, as they were called, for any purpose except for reservations and for the maintenance of the priests and of the many who were employed with them at Quebec, Montreal and out on the missions. Some of these concessions were never even claimed, as, for instance, the one which Governor de Lauson on April 12, 1656 granted to the "Reverend Fathers of the Society of Jesus", to wit, ten leagues (about thirty miles) square near the Onondaga mission, then south of Manlius and not far east of Syracuse. When under Prime Minister Mercier of Quebec a settlement of the controversy of these estates was finally effected, the Jesuits were content with a small part of the amount awarded, the balance going to the diocesan authorities. This amount was $400,000, in partial compensation for the properties which had been taken over by the British Government on the death of the last Jesuit in Canada, prior to the restoration of the Society.[66]

The personnel of the mission was motley for those who imagine that Jesuits are all men of a mould, stripped of individuality. Lalemant was a profound theologian, as Dr. O'Callaghan assures us, but fond of teaching children and candidates for baptism; "Father of the poor", Mary of the Incarnation styles him. Brébeuf had studied theology enough to qualify for ordination. A very ox for labor, of large physique and ardent temperament, his self-restraint was remarkable. He was in demand by the Indian captains, but he knew how to accommodate himself to file as well as rank. Chastellain never appears prominently in the story of the missions. In the Relation of 1640 he is represented as persistent when a good work was to be done. After eight years in Huronia, illness made him retire, but he spent twenty years thereafter in Quebec. Du Peron had a gay sense of humor; every letter, or part of a Relation, from his pen is enlivening. Ragueneau impresses by his thoroughness, his matter-of-fact attitude and sternness. Martyrdom was a part of the day's work for him. In his annals for the public, deeds are mentioned, but names scarcely ever. Still when the martyrdoms were over, he gave very precious and very affectionate accounts of them. Le Moyne was a man of romance. He reaped where others sowed, but he also sowed where others reaped abundantly.

Then there was Le Mercier, over thirty years on the mission, twice superior at Quebec, and for a time vicar of Bishop Laval, writer of many Relations of a style all his own. Finally comes Chaumonot, altogether baffling the pen-portrait, imaginative, mystical, over-credulous some say, without proving it, but as hardy in privation as Brébeuf, and credulous to a fault concerning the virtues and merits of all about him. Of the distinctive characters of Jogues, Daniel, Garnier it would be superfluous to speak.

Out from the palisaded enclosure of St. Mary's these men would venture in the autumn to the different villages, almost every one of which had now become a mission centre. They would go as directed by their chief, Lalemant, not, as some imagine, in a spirit of abject or servile obedience — it is impossible to attribute such dispositions to such men—but with one thing only in mind, the saving of souls. The obedience they had been trained to was that of the children of God, given with the utmost liberty and in a spirit of loyalty and allegiance. By their Rule they were just as much under obligation to make known to their superior what they thought of his command, and of their own ability or inability to obey it, as they were to carry it out; or to do something else, should he deem proper to change what he had ordered. The Relations contain numerous instances, the "Journal des Jésuites" especially, of the care with which superiors consulted their men, and considered from every point of view what was best to do and who was most fitted to do it.[67]

A new factor appears in the mission at this time, which engaged the attention of Jogues. He had charge of the laymen occupied at Ste. Marie. As the priests grew in number, their attendants also increased. Among the colonists were young men who had come to New France for trade, but who had become attached to the missionaries, acting as guides, interpreters, messengers, visitors, catechists, nurses and servants. They took the place of lay-brothers. At first they did not engage to serve for any length of time, but gradually they acquired a liking for the work and adopted it permanently. To satisfy their devotion, the Fathers permitted them to bind themselves by vow to the missions, engaging in return to provide for them for life, and to permit them to wear the religious habit. Neither the vow nor the wearing of a habit were approved by the General of the Order, but in 1644 he approved of the contract between mission and *donné*, involving service and provision for life. They were an important adjunct to the missionaries. Of their number were Goupil, Lalande, Couture, Guérin. Jogues with his kindly manner was particularly useful in managing the six *donnés* or oblates then at the new settlement, and the laborers who helped to build palisade and fort. He had charge also of four village missions. One advantage of the new arrangement for the mission became apparent when small-pox broke out among the Indians. Again they railed at the missionaries and threatened them, calling Brébeuf the arch-sorcerer, but this time the Fathers were too remote to suffer this annoyance as they had the two years before. The supreme advantage however was, as Chaumonot states, that in every cabin of the thirty-two villages instructions had been given by the Fathers.[68]

It was now possible to broaden the horizon and field of the missionaries. In 1640 Jogues and Garnier started on a special mission to the Petun Indians, thirty miles to the south-west in the Blue Mountains, between Lakes Huron and Ontario. They were known as Tobacco Indians, because they traded heavily in that commodity. As the braves were usually absent trading or fishing in summer and fall, winter was the only opportune season for such journeys. The two priests had to travel on snow-shoes. They were deserted by their guides. They had to sleep overnight in the woods. When they arrived at the first village they found that their repute for sorcery had preceded them. They were avoided and even abhorred by everyone. They were threatened and ordered out of every village. In none of them could they remain more than two days. Part of Garnier's account of this experience is as follows:

"Here we have at last arrived, thank God, at the farthest and principal village of our district, to which we have given the name of Saint-Pierre et Saint-Paul. Not having been able to find any savage at the village of La Conception to come with us,— the roads being then too bad, for people who are not seeking God,— we were constrained to start alone; taking our good angels for guides. About the middle of the journey, not having been able to find a certain detour which would have led us to some cabins which are a little isolated, we were surprised by night in a fir grove. We were in a damp place, and could not go from it to seek a drier one; we had trouble enough to pick up some pieces of wood to make a little fire, and some dry branches to lie down upon; the snow was threatening to put out our fire, but it suddenly ceased. God be blessed, we spent the night very quietly. The next morning we came across some poor cabins in the fields, but they had no corn. Finding company there to come into the country with, we were not willing to lose it, because the roads were very difficult on account of the newly-fallen snows, which had obliterated the trails. Accordingly, we set out, and went by many bad roads, at a very bad season, to a little village which we named St. Thomas; we made easily a league by the mere light of the snow, and arrived about eight o'clock in the evening, with good appetite,— not having eaten all day, save each a morsel of bread. We had no design on that village, rather than on another; but having taken what company of savages there offered, and having followed them, we arrived,— no doubt, where God was leading us, for the salvation of a predestined soul which awaited nothing but our coming, in order to die to all its miseries. While we were at a loss to know whether there was not some person critically ill, a young man came to beg us to go and give some relief to one in his cabin. We go thither, and find a poor woman at the last pass; she was instructed, and happily received with the Faith the grace of baptism; shortly after, she beheld herself in glory. In the whole village there was only that one who had need of our help. We ran to some other little villages, where they told us that there were sick people; we baptized some of them,— Our Lord's sheep are much scattered, hither and yon. We have met some persons who at first indeed relish the Gospel; God grant them the grace to embrace it altogether. We received consolation two or three days ago, seeing that a girl, who came to pledge herself to a young man, having a little later heard mention of God and the pains of hell, went to lie down alone, saying, 'He sees us even at night.'

"On arriving in this village, we knew not that there was a little child of the Neutral Nation, aged five years, whom its parents have recently brought here, where hunger causes them to take refuge; for a long time, it was each day believed that that would be the last of its life. Out of 45 or 50 cabins, without thinking of it, we first visited the one in which was this little stranger, and baptized him; he straightway saw himself out of exile and happy in his native land. Those are the first fruits of this Neutral Nation, and this was the very first one to be sprinkled with the blood of Jesus Christ.

"This whole country is filled with evil reports which are current about us. The children, seeing us arrive at any place, exclaim that famine and disease are coming; some women flee, others hide their children from us; almost all refuse us the hospitality which they grant even to the most unknown tribes. We have not been able to find a house for Our Lord,— not having been able to find any place where we can say Mass. Our host,— who is the chief captain of this country, and who through a natural prudence had appeared quite peaceable,— on seeing us pray to God mornings and evenings on our knees, finally could not refrain, on one occasion, from revealing to us what he had on his heart. He begins, therefore, to speak, but in a council voice,— that is to say, loud and distinct: 'Truly, it is now that I fear and speak. What are now these demons but spells to make us die, and finish what the disease has left over, in this cabin? They had told me, indeed, that these were sorcerers, but I believe it too late. This is a thing unknown — that persons who come to lodge at one's house pass the night in postures to which our eyes are nowise accustomed.' Imagine with what looks they regard us in a cabin where they have such fine ideas of us!—We could hardly tranquilize this mind again. They treat us very ill, in order to oblige us to leave. It is, in sooth, all, if we have what suffices for life,— our hunger usually attends us from morning till evening; but these simple people do not see that what retains us here is more precious than all that they conceive in the way of pleasures in this world. There is hardly any corn in this village, and, nevertheless, every day some Attiouandarons arrive (they are those of the Neutral Nation),— bands of men, women, and children, all pale and disfigured, whom famine drives hither. Fleeing famine, they here find death, or rather a blessed life, for we see to it that not one dies without baptism. Among these people was a little child of one year who seemed rather a monster than a human being. It was happily baptized; God, it seems, preserved its life only by miracle, so that, being washed in the blood of Jesus Christ, it might bless His mercies forever.

"While we try to render some honor to God, the devil continues to be adored; even yesterday, in our cabin, they made him a solemn sacrifice. All the people being assembled there, they repeatedly threw tobacco and fat into the fire, making several invocations; and all that for the cure of a wretch whom his private demon afflicts with a certain disease, because he has not obeyed him in the matter of some feasts which he had commanded him.

"Is it a wonder that we are held in abomination
at a place where the devils are acknowledged as
masters? Our host orders that his door be barri-
caded every evening, fearing lest they do us some
violence by night; for, if they killed us in his house,
he would have the reproaches to bear for it, even
from those who desire naught but our death. It
is not this which assures us; we have a more powerful protection, although less visible to these poor
infidels."[69]

Their journey was a failure, but they knew well
the fickle character of the natives. Next year
Garnier would go there and establish a flourishing
mission of the Apostles, and soon it would have
nine stations, with an apostle's name for each. In
1649 he would die a martyr there.

These long-distance explorations became more
frequent, now that the missionaries had provided
for the home missions, and were free to move about.
They were always in winter time. The "Relation"
of 1640 tells of the journey of Jogues and Raymbault as far as Sault Sainte Marie. They had been
invited by Ojibways from that region, who had
come over to the Ottawas to celebrate a Feast of
the Dead. This consisted in gathering together
the departed of all their villages for the ten years
previous and interring them in one great pit. It
was a solemn occasion for the Indians, and they
were religiously disposed. Jogues and his companion had to travel two hundred and fifty miles

for the most part along the northern shore of Lake Huron. Two thousand Indians greeted them and urged them to remain there. All they could do was make known the Faith and plant a great cross facing the Far West to which their successors would go in after years.[70] Raymbault's health was broken by this journey and he died the year following in Quebec. It was the report of this exploration which led Le Jeune to suggest that the vast fresh-water sea Jogues and Raymbault discovered, Lake Superior, might be the coveted route to China![71]

Brébeuf and Chaumonot visited the Neuters, north of Lake Erie, with their forty villages and twelve thousand people, starting in November, 1641. They were also deserted by their guides, and as ill-received as Jogues and Garnier by the Petuns. They were fortunate in finding a leader and they were so persuaded that encouraging voices were leading them, that they determined to call this the Mission of the Angels. They were treated as lepers; the very road they walked over was avoided as infected. They were threatened with death. A council was summoned to decide their fate. Brébeuf went boldly into it, and then retired with his companion to await the verdict. Three times it was adverse. The fourth ballot was favorable, but on condition they would leave the country. It was about this time Brébeuf had a foresight of what was to happen later to his cherished mission among the Hurons. It came to him in the form of a huge cross, which had its stem in the heart of the Iroquois country and its arms overshadowing Huronia. "The cross was large enough to bear all the missionaries among the Hurons."[72]

They spent three hard winter months in this way, permitted only to visit the sick, some of whom they baptized. Heavy snows detained them for twenty-five days on their homeward journey. They were harbored in a cabin by a woman of kindly manners, who with her children ministered to them, but would not listen to their instruction. Brébeuf fell and broke his shoulder-blade soon after leaving the cabin and he had to struggle painfully over ice and through jungle until they reached home on St. Joseph's Day. His report of this expedition is a model of observation in ethnology.[73] For eighteen months he suffered from this fall, until in the summer of 1641 he was called to Quebec for rest and medical attention. Here at last, after seven strenuous years, he could witness consoling evidences of religion. His own brethren had three establishments: one at Sillery for the Indians who were gradually becoming Christian; one at Notre Dame des Anges for the French colonists; and the school for young people, which was started in 1632, developed into a college in 1636, and was provided with suitable buildings in 1647. The work of the Ursulines and Hospital Sisters would also interest him, like as it was to similar works which he had seen in France. He had the gratification of converting two prominent Hurons who had been enemies of religion in Huronia. It was a well-deserved Sabbatical year of rest. His next such year would crown his labor with an everlasting rest. Jogues would soon pass his first year off the mission in far different surroundings. Each would have time to ponder over the problems of the missions, and one question that would interest them was; why so few Christians among the Indians after such long and arduous labor?

This problem was perplexing then. It is not so now. Cardinal Newman remarks that God's hand is not seen in events until they are over, and that is why memory of the past is always so consoling for the Church and for its individual members.[74] The missionaries very properly would admit no adult to baptism without due instruction and without due trial also in constancy. They knew the fickle nature of their people, and they knew also the vicious surroundings in which the newly-converted would have to live. It required nothing short of heroism for tribesman or woman to become a consistent member of the Church. That was the first obstacle to numerous conversions. There was also the difficulty of language. No matter how adept the missionary would become in the use of any tongue, he had to coin new words for most of the things he needed to convey to the Indian mind, so lacking were their languages in terms to express Divine and spiritual facts or thoughts.

It was hard also to acquire the confidence of a people who believed the strangers were the cause of their misfortunes, and who were confirmed in that belief by settlers from other lands than France. The Hurons as a tribe were in no mood to try new things. Famished by drought, decimated by disease, frightened by what they considered the magic of Brébeuf and his associates, they clung all the more fiercely to their own superstitious rites, and indulged in the tribal vices of drinking, gambling, lascivious dancing and other immoralities. In these evil habits the missionaries felt that they were face to face with the demons of hell. Still they never gave up.

The first adult to be baptized in 1637, was followed by over eighty, two years later, and by sixty in 1641. That was little enough, but it proved that genuine conversion was not impossible. The missionaries knew they were doing the work of God. They recalled what their fellow-Jesuits had done and were doing in every part of the world, how in Bordeaux, for instance, within seventeen years (1572–1589), they reduced the Huguenots from seven thousand to an inappreciable number;[75] how one hundred thousand in Paraguay had become Christians after six years of labor on the part of the Jesuit Ruiz de Montoya. Their keen joy over one baptism, even of an infant, suggests also their keen disappointment with the few adults in health they could convert. They were sowing in labor and in sorrow. They all agreed that something more than the ordinary dews of grace was required to fertilize such an arid soil. Among themselves they repeated the adage as old as the Church: The blood of martyrs is the seed of Christians. How could it be verified in this instance? Happy as they all were to live a life that had continual martyrdom, as Jerome Lalemant termed it, not one of them would presume to believe himself worthy of being chosen as the victim. Lalemant had the good sense to say in his "Relation" for 1639: "But if some one asks when we shall execute this great plan [for converting the Hurons],— seeing that hardly have we yet made a beginning, or advanced one step in these countries since we have been here,— my answer to this question is, first, that even if this is not to be accomplished until shortly before the end of the world, yet it is always necessary to begin before ending. . . ."[76]

"We have sometimes wondered whether we could hope for the conversion of this country without the shedding of blood; the principle received, it seems, in the Church of God, that the blood of martyrs is the seed of Christians, made me at one time conclude that this was not to be expected,— yea, that it was not even to be desired; considering the glory that redounds to God from the constancy of the martyrs, with whose blood all the rest of the earth has been so lately drenched, it would be a sort of curse if this quarter of the world should not participate in the happiness of having contributed to the splendor of this glory."[77]

Two at least of the missionaries were praying constantly to have a share in the glory of suffering, if not of martyrdom. Every morning when communicating at the sacrifice of the Mass, Brébeuf repeated the vow which he had made when an exile from the missions, in France. Jogues often made a similar prayer. When in the summer of 1642, he was ordered down to Quebec to obtain relief for the mission, which was then in destitute condition, he went one day into the chapel, bent in prayer to the ground, beseeching Our Lord to grant him the favor of suffering for His glory. Engraved in the depths of his soul was the answer: "Thy prayer is heard. What thou hast asked is granted. Be courageous and steadfast". He was soon to enter on his suffering, but not yet as a martyr.

CHAPTER TWELVE
An Era of Martyrdom

Distress in Huronia—Jogues leads relief expedition—Captured by Mohawks—Two-week trail in torture—Gruesome village spectacle—A year in slavery—A Martyr's Confessions—Goupil, first victim—Death for the Sign of the Cross—A martyr's interment.

HURONIA was in distress. The mission itself was in great need. Harvests had been poor. Illness abounded. Clothing was scarce. The new mission stations needed vestments and altar-ware. Quebec was the only source of supplies. Raymbault's illness required him to go there, but some one must accompany him. The Iroquois were on the warpath. They were willing to make peace with the French, but not with the Hurons or Algonquins. The route lay through the villages of both. Jogues was chosen to lead the expedition. He started early in June, 1642, arriving safely about mid-July. It took about two weeks for his Indian companions to transact business and see what was of interest. Many of them were Christians, or preparing to be. They would naturally wish to see the Indian Catholic settlement at Sillery, the convents, hospitals, and churches. The Fathers encouraged this, as it was an object lesson which impressed on them the strength and dignity of religion.

[152]

Isaac Jogues

THE JESUIT MARTYRS

On August 1st he started homeward with about forty in the company, four of them Frenchmen, the canoes heavily laden with goods for the Mission. They were scarcely a day on the way when they were ambushed and taken captive by the Iroquois. The story of their ill-treatment, torture, captivity, and, in some instances, death has been frequently told, but never more impressively than by the principal victim, Jogues. Comment or paraphrase would spoil it. It is more like the "Confessions" of St. Augustine than a description of torture. Usually those who attempt to repeat the story in their own words apologize fastidiously for depicting such revolting cruelty. The language of Jogues lifts the imagination above gross details and centres the attention more on his own spiritual elevation than on his bodily suffering. His letter was written to his provincial, or chief superior, in France. It is dated from the Mohawk village then located near the site of the present village of Auriesville, New York. To appreciate its contents one need only recall that the Iroquois were the fiercest Indian tribes in the east at that time, that they were bitterly opposed to the French, implacable to the Hurons, hateful of the Black Robe, as the missionary was called on account of his clerical garment. There were five tribes or nations, Mohawks, Onondagas, Oneidas, Cayugas and Senecas, situated in this order along the Mohawk Valley, between Schenectady and Lake Erie. They numbered about twenty-five thousand and had twenty-five hundred warriors. The Auriesville village was the easternmost, and it was there Jogues was tortured and kept in captivity for fourteen months. It was near there he wrote what follows of this chapter, being at the time in the Dutch settlement Rensselaerswyck, now Albany.

"Letter from Father Isaac Jogues to his Provincial Jean Filleau.

[dated August 5, 1643.]

"When desiring to write to Your Reverence, the first doubt that I had was, in which language I ought to do so,— Latin or French; then, having almost forgotten them both, I found equal difficulty in each. Two reasons have moved me to use Latin. The first, for the sake of being able sometimes to employ certain sentences from the Sacred Scripture, from which I have received great consolation in my adversities. The second, because I desire that this letter may not be too common. Your Reverence's great charity will excuse, as it has done at other times, my failings; especially since for eight years now I have been living among barbarians, not only in usages, but also in a costume similar to theirs. But I fear 'that I am unskilled in speech and in knowledge'; not knowing the precious time 'of my visitation': first, then, I beg you, if this letter shall come unto your hands, to aid me with your Holy Sacrifices. and prayers by the whole Province,— as being among people no less barbarous by birth than in manners. And I hope you will do this gladly, when you shall have seen by this letter the obligation under which I am to God, and my need of spiritual help.

"We started from the Hurons on the 13th of June, 1642, with four canoes and twenty-three persons — eighteen barbarians, and five Frenchmen. The journey — besides the difficulties, especially of portages,— was dangerous by reason of the enemies, who, seizing every year the highways, take many prisoners; and I know not how Father Jean de Brébeuf escaped them last year. They, being incensed against the French, had shortly before declared that, if they should capture any one of them, they would, besides the other torments, burn him alive by a slow fire. The Superiors, aware of the dangers of this journey,— necessary, however, for the glory of God,— spoke to me of them, adding that they did not oblige me thereto. But I did not gainsay them, 'nor have I gone back'. I embraced with good courage that obedience put before me for the glory of God; and if I had excused myself, some one else, of greater ability, would have been substituted in my place, with more detriment to the mission. We made the journey not without fear, dangers, losses, and shipwrecks, and, thirty-five days after our departure, we arrived safe and sound at the residence of Three Rivers; due thanks being there rendered to God, we spent twenty-five days partly there, partly at Kebek, according to necessity. Having finished our business, and celebrated the feast of our holy Father Ignatius, we embarked again on the first of August for the Hurons. On the second day of our journey, some of our men discovered on the shore fresh tracks of people who had passed there,— without knowing whether or not they were enemies. Eustache Ahatsistari, famous and experienced in war, believes them enemies. 'But, however strong they may be deemed,' he says, 'they are not more than three canoes; and therefore we have nothing to fear.' We then continue the journey. But, a mile beyond, we meet them to the number of seventy, in twelve canoes, concealed in the grass and woods. They suddenly surround us, and fire their arquebuses, but without wounding us. The Hurons, terrified, abandon the canoes, and many flee to the deepest part of the woods; we were left alone, we four Frenchmen, with a few others, Christians and catechumens, to the number of twelve or fourteen. Having commended themselves to God, they stand on the defensive; but, being quickly overwhelmed by numbers, and a Frenchman named René Goupil, who was fighting among the first, being captured with some Hurons, they ceased from the defense. I, who was barefoot, would not and could not flee,— not willing, moreover, to forsake a Frenchman and the Hurons, who were partly captured without baptism, partly near being the prey of the enemies, who were seeking them in the woods. I therefore stayed alone at the place where the skirmish had occurred, and surrendered myself to the man who was guarding the prisoners, that I might be made their companion in their perils, as I had been on the journey. He was amazed at what I did, and approached, not without fear, to place me with them. I forthwith rejoiced with the Frenchman over the grace which the Lord was showing us: I roused him to constancy, and heard him in confession. After the Hurons had been instructed in the Faith, I baptized them; and as the number increased, my occupation of instructing and baptizing them also increased. There was finally led in among the captives the valiant Eustache Ahatsistari, a Christian; who seeing me, said: 'I praise God that He has granted me what I so much desired,— to live and die with thee.' I knew not what to answer, being oppressed with compassion, when Guillaume Cousture also came up, who had come with me from the Hurons. This man, seeing the impossibility of longer defending himself, had fled with the others into the forests; and, as he was a young man not only of courageous disposition, but strong in body, and fleet in running, he was already out of the grasp of the one who was pursuing him. But, having turned back, and seeing that I was not with him, 'I will not forsake,' he said to himself, 'my dear Father alone in the hands of enemies;' and immediately returning to the barbarians, he had of his own accord become a prisoner. Oh, that he had never taken such a resolution! It is no consolation in such cases to have companions of one's misfortunes. But who can prevent the sentiment of charity? Such is the feeling toward us of those laymen who, without any worldly interest, serve God and aid us in our ministrations among the Hurons. This one had slain, in the fight, one of the most prominent among the enemies; he was therefore treated most cruelly. They stripped him naked, and, like mad dogs, tore off his nails with their teeth, bit his fingers, and pierced his right hand with a javelin; but he suffered it all with invincible patience,— remembering the nails of the Savior, as he told me afterward. I embraced him with great affection, and exhorted him to offer to God those pains, for himself and for those who tormented him. But those executioners although admiring me at the beginning, soon afterward grew fierce, and, assailing me with their fists and with knotty sticks, left me half dead on the ground, and a little later, having carried me back to where I was, they also tore off my nails, and bit with their teeth my two forefingers, causing me incredible pain. They did the same to René Goupil,— leaving unharmed the Hurons, who were now made slaves. Then, having brought us all together again, they made us cross the river, where they divided among themselves the spoil — that is, the riches of the poor Hurons, and what they carried, which was church utensils, books, etc., things very precious to us. Meanwhile, I baptized some who had not yet received that rite,— and, among others, an old man of eighty years, who, having had orders to embark with the others, said: 'How shall I, who am already decrepit, go into a distant and foreign country?' Refusing, then, to do so, he was slain at the same place where he had been baptized,— losing the life of the body where he had received that of the soul. Thence, with shouts proper to conquerors, they depart, to conduct us into their countries, to the number of twenty-two captives, besides three of our men already killed. We suffered many hardships on the journey, wherein we spent thirty-eight days amid hunger, excessive heat, threats, and blows,— in addition to the cruel pains of our wounds, not healed, which had putrefied, so that worms dropped from them. They, besides, even went to far — a savage act — as in cold blood to tear out our hair and beards, wounding us with their nails, which are extremely sharp, in the most tender and sensitive parts of the body. I do not mention the inward pains caused at the sight of that funereal pomp of the oldest and most excellent Christians of the new Church of the Hurons, who often drew the tears from my eyes, in the fear lest these cruelties might impede the progress of the Faith still incipient there. On the eighth day of our journey, we met two hundred barbarians, who were going to attack the French at the fort which they were building at Richelieu; these, after their fashion, thinking to exercise themselves in cruelty, and thus to derive prosperous results from their wars, wished to travel with us. Thanks being then rendered to the sun, which they believe to preside in wars, and their muskets being fired as a token of rejoicing, they made us disembark, in order to receive us with heavy blows of sticks. I, who was the last, and therefore more exposed to these beatings, fell, midway in the journey which we were obliged to make to a hill, on which they had erected a stage; and I thought that I must die there, because I neither could, nor cared to, arise. What I suffered, is known to One for Whose love and cause it is a pleasant and glorious thing to suffer. Finally, moved by a cruel mercy,— wishing to conduct me alive to their country,— they ceased beating me, and conducted me, half dead, to the stage,— all bleeding from the blows which they had given me, especially in the face. Having come down from it, they loaded me with a thousand insults, and with new blows on the neck and on the rest of the body. They burned one of my fingers, and crushed another with their teeth; and the others, already bruised and their sinews torn, they so twisted that even at present, although partly healed, they are crippled and deformed. A barbarian twice took me by the nose, to cut it off; but this was never allowed him by that Lord Who willed that I should still live,—

for the savages are not wont to give life to persons enormously mutilated. We spent there much of the night, and the rest of it passed not without great pain, and without food, which even for many days we had hardly tasted. Our pains were increased by the cruelties which they practised upon our Christians,— especially upon Eustache, both of whose thumbs they cut off; and, through the midst of the wound made on his left hand they thrust a sharp skewer, even to the elbow, with unspeakable pain; but he suffered it with the same — that is, invincible — constancy. The day following, we encountered other canoes, which were likewise going to war; those people then cut off some fingers from our companions; not without our own fear. On the tenth day, in the afternoon, we left the canoes, in order to make the remainder of the four days' journey on foot. To the customary severities was added a new toil, to carry their goods, although herein they treated me better than I expected,— whether because I could not, or whether because I retained in captivity itself, and near to death, a spirit haply too proud. Hunger accompanied us always; we passed three days without any food, but on the fourth we found some wild fruits. I had not provided myself sufficiently when we abandoned the canoes, for fear lest my body should be too robust and vigorous in the fire and in the torments, not to dissimulate 'about my infirmities'. On the second day, they put a kettle on the fire, as if to prepare something to eat; but there was nothing in it but warm water, which each one was allowed to drink at his pleasure. Finally, on the 18th day, the eve of the Assumption of the Most Blessed Virgin, we arrived at the first village of the Hiroquois. I thanked the Lord that, on the day on which the Christians celebrate so solemn a feast, He had called us to share His pains. We had anticipated that day as truly bitter and calamitous; and it had been easy for René Goupil and for me to avoid it, because often, when unbound about mid-night, we were able to flee,— with the hope, if not of returning to ours, at least of dying more easily in the woods. But he refused to do so, and I would rather suffer every pain than abandon my French and Huron Christians to death, and deprive them of the consolation which they could receive from a priest at that time. So, on the eve of the Assumption, about the twentieth hour, we arrived at the river which flows past their village. Here were awaiting us, on both banks of the river, the old Huron slaves and the Hiroquois, the former to warn us that we should flee, for that otherwise we would be burned; the latter to beat us with sticks, fists, and stones, as before,— especially my head, because they hate shaven and short hair. Two nails had been left me; they tore these out with their teeth, and tore off that flesh which is under them, with their very sharp nails, even to the bone. We remained there, exposed to their taunts a few moments; then they led us to the village situated on another hill. Before arriving, we met the young men of the country, in a line, armed with sticks, as before; but we, who knew that, if we had separated ourselves from the number of those who are scourged, we would be separated from the number of the sons, 'for He scourgeth every son whom He receiveth', offered ourselves with ready will to our God, Who became paternally cruel to the end that He might take pleasure in us, as in His sons. We went one by one. First there walked a Frenchman, altogether naked; René was in the middle; I the last, in shirt and trousers. The Hiroquois had placed themselves between us and the Hurons, in order to moderate our pace, for the sake of giving time to any one who struck us. A long time, and cruelly, 'the wicked have wrought upon my back', —not only with sticks, but also with iron rods, which they have from the Dutch; and one of the first, with a piece of iron thick as a fist, attached to a rope, gave us each a blow so fierce that I would have fallen half dead, if the fear of another like blow had not given me strength to pass on. We hardly had strength to reach the stage erected in the middle of the village. René, who was not very nimble, received so many blows, especially in the face, that nothing was seen of him but the whites of his eyes, all the more beautiful, since more like that one, 'as it were a leper and as one struck by God, in whom there is neither beauty nor comeliness'. Hardly did we breathe upon the stage when, with a great rod, we were three times struck on the bare shoulders; and they began to unsheathe knives, in order to cut off the rest of our fingers. Because they esteemed me the most, they began with me, whom they saw respected by the French and the Hurons. There approach me then an old man and a woman, whom he orders to cut off my thumb; at first she refuses, but being, as it were, compelled three or four times by the old man, she finally does so. This woman was an Algonquin,—a Christian slave, captured a few months before,— and her name was Jeanne. What consolation to suffer at the hands of those for whom one dies rather than abandon them to visible and invisible enemies. Then I, taking with my other hand the amputated thumb, offered it to Thee, O my Living and True God,— mindful of the sacrifices which I had offered Thee in Thy Church,— until, admonished by one of my companions, I let it fall, for fear that they might put it in my mouth, in order to make me swallow it as they often do. As for René, they cut off his right thumb at the first joint. I thank God that they left me the one on my right hand, so that by this letter I may pray my Fathers and brethren to offer prayers for us in the Holy Church of God. Unto her we are recommended with a twofold and new title, since she is accustomed to pray 'for the afflicted and captives'. The following day, the feast of the

Blessed Virgin,— after having kept us till noon
on the stage, they conducted us to another village,
five or six miles distant from the first; and the
barbarians who was leading me took away my shirt,
leaving me nothing,— except a rag, which he could
not deny to decency,— but a piece of sacking,
which I myself asked from him, in order to cover
my shoulders. But these, bent with so many beatings, refused to sustain that rough and rude weight,
especially after a burning sun roasted my skin as
in an oven,— on account of which, shortly afterward, that of the neck, the shoulders, and the arms,
being burned, fell off. At the entrance to this
village, they did not omit — although contrary to
their custom — to beat us once again, with blows
the more atrocious in proportion as the multitude
did not hinder them from measuring them; they
struck us especially on the bones of the legs, with
what pain may be imagined. The rest of the
day we remained upon the stage; at night, in a
cabin, naked on the bare ground, bound with chains,
exposed to the revilings of each sex and of every
age. They threw coals and live ashes on our bare
flesh,— which, for us who were bound, it was difficult to throw off. We remained there two days and
two nights, almost without eating or sleeping,—
tormented further by the sight of the torments
which they inflicted upon our Huron companions,
whose wrists they bound so tightly with cords that
they fainted therefrom. I regarded these as my

spiritual sons, shortly before regenerated to God by holy baptism,— that is to say, with the bowels of a Father, to whom love served as executioner. I consoled them, however, with the words of the Apostle: 'Do not therefore lose your confidence, which hath a great reward. Through many tribulations we must enter the Kingdom of God. You shall lament and weep', etc., 'but your sorrow will be turned into joy. A woman, when she is in labor, hath sorrow, but remembereth no more the anguish, for joy', etc. In a word, 'for that which is at present momentary and light of our tribulation, worketh for us an eternal weight of glory'. The stages of the barbarians had not yet seen either Frenchmen or Christian Hurons: to satisfy, then, the curiosity of all, we were led everywhere. At the third village, we entered with great peace, but not without pain, since we met there four other Hurons freshly captured, and mutilated like us. I found means of instructing in the Faith and baptizing these prisoners,— two upon the stage itself, with the dew, which I found quite abundant in the great leaves of Turkish corn, the stalks of which they gave us to chew; the other two on the journey to another village, at a brook which we encountered by the way. Here the rain and the cold made our nakedness more keenly felt; therefore, trembling with cold, I sometimes went down from the stage in order to warm myself in some cabin, but I was forthwith led back to it. To cut off Guillaume's

right forefinger, a barbarian used, not a knife, but
a shell, like a saw; which could not cut the tough
and slippery sinews; and therefore he tore it off
by sheer force, which caused the sufferer's arm to
swell even to the elbow. A certain person, out of
pity, received him into a hut during those two days
that we stayed there,— not without anxiety on my
side, as I knew not where he was. At night, they
led us into a cabin, where they commanded us to
sing, as was their wont. It is necessary to obey
and to sing, 'but of the canticles of the Lord in a
land of exile'. From singing they came to torments,
especially in the case of René and me; they burned
me with coals and live ashes, especially on the
breast; and they bound me upright between two
stakes, set between the shoulders and the elbow,
with two pieces of bark, wherewith they often
bind those whom they burn, so that I thought that
I was to be burned. And — that you may know
that, if I endured the rest with strength and with
patience, it was not my own courage, but that of
Him 'Who giveth strength to the weary'— in that
torture, being almost left to myself alone, I wept
('I will glory in the things that concern my infirmity'); and, on account of the great pain, I begged
that they would not tie me so tightly. But it so
happened that the Lord permitted that, the more
I besought Him, the more they bound me. They
kept me thus about a quarter of an hour, then they
loosed me; otherwise, I would have swooned. I

thank Thee, O good Jesus, because I have learned
with some little experience what Thou didst con-
descend to suffer for me on the Cross, where Thy
most holy body was not even sustained with cords,
but hung by Thy hands and feet, transfixed with
hardest nails. For spending the rest of the night,
they bound us on the earth to several stakes; and
what did they not do to us, or try to do? But
again I thank You, O Lord, that You kept me pure
from the impure hands of the barbarians. Two
days later, they led us to the second village, in
order to take final counsel concerning us. Now for
seven days they had been leading us from village
to village, from stage to stage,— being made a
spectacle to God and to the angels, the contempt
and sport of the barbarians,— when finally we
were notified of death by fire — news assuredly full
of horror, but softened by the thought of the Divine
Will, and by the hope of a better life. I spoke for
the last time, as I believed, to the French and the
Hurons to animate them by reminding them of the
sufferings of that One 'Who bore with such contradiction from sinners against Himself', of the brevity
of the torments, and the eternity of the glory, etc.
I also admonished them, especially Eustache, that
in the torments they should look at me, and made
some sign, so that I might bestow on them the
last absolution, as I did in his case, repeatedly; but
the French and almost all the other Hurons were
granted life. The fortitude of this man was

marvelous; and — whereas the others, while in the
fire, are wont to have the sentiment and use the
words of him who said, 'may an avenger arise from
our ashes', he, with Christian spirit, entreated the
Hurons present, that the thought of his death
should never prejudice the peace of the Hiroquois.
They also killed Paul Onnonhoaraton, a young
man of about twenty-five years, of great courage,
who laughed at death,— being animated with the
hope of a better life, as he publicly declared. This
man, on the journey, when the Hiroquois were
coming to torment me, offered himself for me,
begging them that they should rather exercise
cruelty toward him. God will have rewarded him
for that notable charity wherewith 'he gave his life
for his friends', who amid bonds had begotten him
for Christ. Guillaume was given to a Hiroquois
family. When they spare the life of any slave,
they usually receive him into some family in the
place of some dead kinsman, whom the slave is said
to bring to life again, by taking the name and the
same degree of relationship; so that they call him,
like the dead man, 'father', 'brother', 'son', etc.
But, in the case of René and myself, because we
were not so strong, the final decision was not taken,
but they left us together, as it were, in a free
slavery. Therein, as being half idle, we began to
feel more keenly the pains of unhealed wounds,
irritated by a thousand annoying little creatures,
from which our mutilated fingers did not permit us

to defend ourselves. We observed, by necessity more than convenience, that aphorism, 'the food is not good for the sick',— especially René, who was not accustomed to the Turkish corn without salt. This diet perhaps availed to effect that, in the space of three weeks, we began to use our hands. Meanwhile, those two hundred returned, whom we had encountered on the journey,— overcome by the French in lesser number, who were commanded by the Chevalier de Montmagni, governor of the country, whom they were intending to surprise. On this account, it again began to be a question of killing us; but we know not how God prevented the execution of this threat. On the day of the Nativity of the Blessed Virgin, one of the principal persons among the Dutch, who have a colony about forty miles distant from the barbarians, came to treat for our ransom. He spent several days there, and offered much, but obtained nothing,— the barbarians, in order not to offend him, feigning, by way of excuse, that they would conduct us back to the French. Perhaps the leaders had some such intention; but, at the final council which assembled for this affair, the crowd and those who were most turbulent, prevented its accomplishment. Indeed, if by special Providence of God we had not been outside the village when the council was ended, they would have killed us; but, having sought us awhile in vain, they finally returned each one to his own village. René and I having gone back, and been warned of the danger, we withdrew without, toward a hill, in order to perform our devotions with more liberty; we offered our lives to God, and began the rosary of the Blessed Virgin. We were at the fourth decade when we met two young men, who commanded us to return to the village. 'This encounter', I said to René, 'is not auspicious, especially in these circumstances. Let us commend ourselves to God and to the Blessed Virgin.' In fact, at the gate of the village one of these two draws a hatchet, which he has kept concealed, and strikes René's head with it. He fell, half dead, but remembered, according to the agreement made between us, to invoke the most Holy Name of Jesus, in order to obtain indulgence. I, expecting a like blow, uncover myself, and cast myself on my knees; but the barbarian, having left me a little time thus, commanded me to rise, saying he had not permission to kill me, as I was under the protection of another family. I then arise, and give the last absolution to my dear companion, who still breathed, but whose life the barbarian finally took away with two more blows. He was not more than thirty-five years of age; he was a man of unusual simplicity and innocence of life, of invincible patience, and very conformable to the Divine Will. He was worthy to be acknowledged by Your Reverence as yours, not only because he had been, with credit, for several months in our novitiate, but also because here he had consecrated himself, under obedience to the Superiors of the Society, in the service of our neophytes and catechumens,— to whom with the art of surgery he was of great assistance; and finally, because, a few days before, he had consecrated himself with the vows. The long prayers that he made had rendered him odious to the barbarians, who for this reason esteemed him a sorcerer; but the sign of the cross, which he often made on the brows of the children, was the last and true cause of his death,—an old man, grandfather of one of them, having ordered the murderer to chastise with death the Frenchman's superstition, as practised on the person of one of his descendants; and I learned this from the child's mother, and from many others of the country. But I was given to another master, who hated us mortally; in consequence, they believed so surely that he would kill me, that he who had lent me that wherewith to cover myself, asked it from me again, in order not to lose it at my death. I did not fail, however, on the following day, to seek, even at the peril of my life, the body of the deceased, for the sake of burying it. They had tied a rope to his neck, and dragged him naked through the whole village, and had then thrown him into the river, at some distance away. My first master warned me to withdraw, if I did not wish to be killed like him; but I, who was weary of that manner of living, would have reckoned it great gain to die in the exercise of a work of mercy.

I then pursued my journey, and, with the guidance and aid of a man of the country,— furnished me for escort by the same person who, out of friendship, was dissuading me from going thither,— I found him by the bank of the river, half eaten by the dogs; and there, at the bottom of a dry torrent, I cover him with stones, intending to return thither the following day alone, with a pickaxe, in order to bury him securely. I found, at my return, two armed young men, who were awaiting me to conduct me, as they said, to another village,— but, really, to kill me in some retired place. I told them I could not follow them without orders from my master, who would not consent. It was necessary to hinder, on the following day, another, who had come for this purpose, from seeking me in a field,— the Lord causing me to see by experience that He was the protector of my life without Whom a hair of our head will not perish. On the following day, I return to the place with tools, but they had taken away my brother. I go again, I seek everywhere, and I myself go into the river up to my waist,— although it was swollen by the night's rains, and cold, since it was the month of October. I seek him with my hands and with my feet; they tell me that the high water has removed him elsewhere. I hold obsequies for him as best I can, singing the psalms and prayers thereto appointed by the Church; I mingle my tears with the water of the torrent; I groan and sigh. I can gain no news of him before the following spring, when, the snows being melted, the young men of the country notify me that they have seen his bones on the same bank of the river; these, together with the head, having reverently kissed, I then finally buried as best I could".[78]

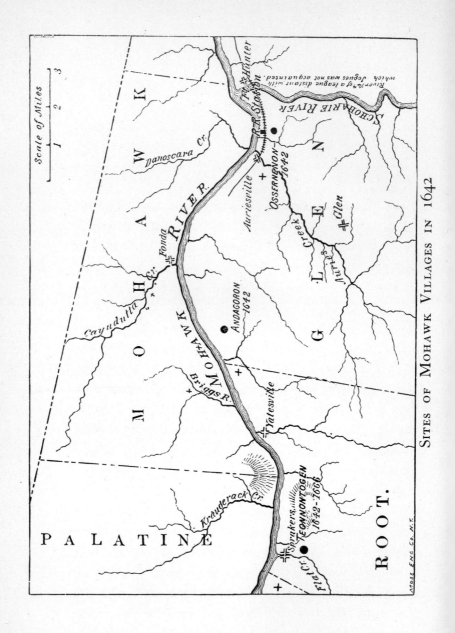

Scale of Miles

1 2 3

M O H A W K   R I V E R.

Danoscara Cr.

Cayudutta Cr.

Fonda

Briggs R.

Krauderack Cr.

Sprakers

Flat Cr.

P A L A T I N E

Auriesville

ANDAGORON
1642

Yatesville

TEONNONTOGEN
1642-1666

Fort Hunter

Ft. Stacton

OSSERNENON
1642

SCHOHARIE RIVER

River ¼ of a league distant with
which Jogues was not acquainted.

G L E N

Glen

Auries Creek

R O O T.

Moss Eng. Co. N.Y.

SITES OF MOHAWK VILLAGES IN 1642

CHAPTER THIRTEEN

An Apostle in Slavery

The Dutch intervene—A slave on the Mohawk—The winter's hunt—A snow-bound oratory—Life in the balance—His friends among the Dutch—Final decision to seek freedom—Reformed Minister and Jesuit—Reception at New Amsterdam—Return to France—Return to Canada—Back to the Mohawks—Death.

AS soon as news of the torture of Jogues and his companions reached the Dutch fort, Arendt van Corlaer, the commandant, Jean Labatie, his interpreter, and Jacob Jansen of New Amsterdam (now New York), went as ambassadors to the Mohawk village in order to obtain their release. This was on September 7. They were unsuccessful. The Indians pretended they would give the prisoners their liberty, but they did not keep their word. Jogues and Goupil became slaves. The other captives were distributed among the villagers farther west. As Jogues relates in his narrative, René Goupil was tomahawked by an Indian on September 29th for having made the sign of the Cross and taught it to some children.

Jogues was then adopted by the Wolf Clan, one of the three families or divisions of the tribe, the others being known as the Bear and the Turtle. He was given over to a family who had lost a son in war. His life was in constant danger. Several times attempt was made to decoy him beyond the village in order to kill him. His master, who alone had right of life and death over him, warned him of his danger. He, therefore, after attending to the work of the cabin, making the fires, drawing the water, and cooking, avoided crowded places and spent his time reading and praying. He had saved one book, the letter of St. Paul to the Hebrews, with comments by Godeau. He had a picture of St. Bruno with the device *O Bonitas!* (goodness) and a little wooden cross made by himself. Among the loot of the Indians he found a "Following of Christ" and a Little Office of the Blessed Virgin Mary. These were his consolation. He narrated how in his solitude he had strange dreams, all of them naturally having to do with persecution and crosses.

He constantly recalls that he was born in Orleans where the cathedral bears the name of Holy Cross, and that, therefore, he should be a citizen of the Cross. He learns as much of the language as the Indians permit him to learn. He goes so far as to preach to them and, whenever he can, baptizes children at the point of death. He ministers to the many captives, Algonquins and Hurons, who were in the villages, and sometimes to an unfortunate who was about to undergo torture and death. He accompanies the Indians on their winter hunt, refuses, in spite of his weakness, to partake of the game they got, because they had offered it idolatrously to their god Aireskoi, boldly telling them he would never live on food offered to the Devil. They in turn treated him cruelly. Besides hunger and insult, he had to suffer night and day from the intense cold, having only a wretched skin for covering. His whole consolation was in his remembrance of the Scriptures, which sometimes he repeats word for word, at other times in paraphrases; in fact he was accustomed to think in Biblical terms.

" 'I thought', he writes, 'of my dear companions, whose blood had so lately covered me, and I heard a report that good William had also ended his life in most cruel torments, and that a like end was in store for me on our return to the town. Then the remembrance of my whole life rushed back to me, with all its unfaithfulness to God, and all its faults. I groaned to see myself die "in the midst of my days", as if rejected by the Lord, deprived of the sacraments of the Church, and with no good works to propitiate my Judge. Thus tormented with a desire to live and the fear of death, I groaned, and cried to my God, "When shall my grief and my anguish come to an end? When wilt Thou 'see my abjection and my labor'? When wilt Thou give me 'calm after the storm'? When shall 'my sorrow be turned into joy'?" Then he adds, in a lively sentiment of humility and confidence: 'I should have perished unless the Lord "had shortened the evil days"; but I had recourse to my support and ordinary refuge, the Holy Scriptures, of which I could recall some passages. They taught me to see in God His goodness, and made me alive to the fact that although deprived of all aids of piety, "the just man liveth by faith". I often pondered on these words: "I followed the running waters" to endeavor to quench my thirst. On the law of the Lord I meditated day and night, for "unless Thy law had been my meditation, I had then perhaps perished in my abjection"; and "perhaps the waters had swallowed us up"'.

" 'But "Blessed be the Lord, who hath not given us to be a prey to the teeth" of my enemies, " for now their hour seemed come and the power of darkness". "I was pressed out of measure above my strength, so that I was weary even of life". Meanwhile I repeated with Job, but in another sense, "Although *God* should kill me, I will trust in Him' ".[79]

Jogues built an oratory a short distance from the cabin where he was accustomed to pray, kneeling before a large Cross which he had cut in the bark of a tree. He even made his annual Retreat, or Spiritual Exercises. On the way home from the hunt he had to carry more than his share of the burdens. Crossing a river, a woman and her child fell off the tree-trunk that had been thrown over for a bridge and were drowning, when Jogues plunged in and rescued them. Arriving home, he went from cabin to cabin, begging for something to cover him, not merely because of the cold, but for the sake of decency. Most of the Indians jeered at him, one threw him a rag, but a Dutchman, who was at the village trading, obtained clothes for him. The Indians sent him on long and arduous errands, carrying heavy parcels to members of other villages. They put him to care for a tribesman who was dying of a disease so loathsome that all shunned him. It was precisely what Jogues was happy to do.

Gradually, the mother of his master, and even the master himself, became more kindly disposed to him. They even helped him to learn the language. As the cabin was a resort for the more prominent members of the tribe, he learned many things about them, and took occasion to speak to them about religion. They plainly agreed that he knew the truth, but, like the Hurons, they asked: of what use it would be to them? They left him free to go about the villages, where he could instruct and console many captives. They took him on a fishing expedition over the Saratoga Lake. Difficult as these trips were, Jogues liked them. They afforded him time for greater union with God.

" 'How often in these journeys', he writes, 'and in that quiet wilderness, "did we sit by the rivers of Babylon, and weep while we remembered thee, Sion", not only exulting that Sion in heaven, but even thee, Jerusalem, praising thy God on earth. 'How often, though in a strange land, did we sing the canticle of the Lord', and mountain and wildwood resounded with the praises of their Maker,

12

which from their creation they had never heard!
How often on the stately trees of the forest did I
carve the most sacred name of Jesus, that seeing it
the demons might fly, who tremble when they hear
it! How often, too, did I not strip off the bark to
form on them the Most Holy Cross of the Lord,
that the foe might fly before it, and that by it Thou,
O Lord my King, "mightest reign in the midst of
Thy enemies"—the enemies of Thy cross, the mis-
believers and the pagans who dwell in that land,
and the demons who rule so powerfully there! I
rejoiced, too, that I had been led by the Lord into
the wilderness, at the very time when the Church
recalls the story of His Passion, so that I might
more uninterruptedly remember the course of its
bitterness and gall, and my soul pine away at the
remembrance' ".[80]

Life, however, for a prisoner among the Mohawks
was always precarious. A dream, a foolish suspicion, the report of bad news from traders or warriors who were out of the village, would at any
moment lead the sachems of the tribe to destroy
a victim. As Easter came near it was decided that
he should die, because ten Mohawk warriors who
had been on the warpath for some time had not
been heard of. Everything was prepared. The
torture was to be applied on Good Friday. Unexpectedly a group of Abenaki Indians were brought
in. Five of the men were doomed to torture, the
women and children were consigned to slavery. The

torture of Jogues was forgotten and he was even allowed to prepare the prisoners, whom he succeeded in baptizing before their ordeal began. Not long after three young women and some children were brutally treated and burned to death. Jogues had the consolation of baptizing one, having to rush into the flames to do so. His life was thus spent in witnessing such harrowing scenes and in constant peril of being himself the victim in one of them. Still, in his humility he considered himself in some way responsible for all this evil.

" 'I certainly', says he, 'felt in my own person this punishment deserved for my sins, and pronounced of old by God to His people when He said "their solemnities, their new-moons, and all their festival-times . . . shall be turned into mourning and lamentation", as Easter, and Whitsuntide, and the Nativity of St. John the Baptist each brought sorrows on me, which increased to agony . . . . "Wo is me, wherefore was I born to see the ruin of my people?" Verily, in these and like heart-rending cares, "my life is wasted with grief, and my years with sighs"; "for the Lord hath corrected me for mine iniquity and hath made my soul waste away as a spider". "He hath filled me with bitterness, He hath inebriated me with wormwood"; "because the comforter, the relief of my soul, is far from me"; "but in all these things we overcome", and by the favor of God will overcome, "because of Him that hath loved us", until "He come that is to come, and will not delay"; "until my day like that of a hireling come", or "my change be made" ".[81]

Jogues had good neighbors at Rensselaerswyck, now Albany, where Fort Orange, the Dutch trading outpost, was situated. The Dutch had never ceased to work for his release. The Governor of Quebec, Montmagny, was earnest enough, but negotiation on his part would be futile. He had not the military force to compel a deliverance. Indeed, to attempt this would have immediately resulted in Jogues' torture and death. Not only were the Dutch at Rensselaerswyck concerned about Jogues. The States-General had commanded the Dutch Governor at New Amsterdam to do all in his power to free the prisoner. On his part Jogues was not over eager to obtain his freedom. As he wrote to Governor Montmagny on June 30, 1643, his fourth letter, and his first to arrive at its destination, he begged that he should not be taken into consideration. "Let no sympathy for me prevent your taking any measure that seems to you best fitted to advance the greater glory of God."[82] Soon after he wrote to his Provincial in France that:

" 'Although I could in all probability escape either through the Europeans or the Indian nations around us, did I wish to fly, yet on this cross to which Our Lord has nailed me, with Himself, am I resolved by His grace to live and die. For who in my absence would console the French captives?

Who absolve the penitent? Who remind the
christened Huron of his duty? Who instruct the
prisoners constantly brought in? Who baptize
them dying, encourage them in their torments?
Who cleanse the infants in the saving waters? Who
provide for the salvation of the dying adult, the
instruction of those in health? Indeed I cannot
but think it a peculiar interposition of Divine goodness, that while a nation, fallen from the true
Catholic religion, barred the entrance of the Faith
to these regions on one side, and on the other, a
fierce war between savage nations and, on their
account, with the French, I should have fallen into
the hands of these Indians, who by the will of
God reluctantly, and I may say against their will,
have thus far spared my life, that through me,
though unworthy, those might be instructed, believe,
and be baptized, who are predestined to eternal
life. Since the time when I was taken, I have
baptized seventy persons, children, young people
and old, of five different nations and languages,
that of "every tribe, and people, and tongue, they
might stand in the sight of the Lamb' ".[83]

It is true that he had some extraordinary consolations. On one of his chance excursions with some
tribesmen, he came across the Indian who had
charitably cut the thongs which bound him when
he begged to be taken down from the gibbet to
which they had attached him. He had the satisfaction of baptizing this man. On July 31st he went

with the Indians of the village to Fort Orange to trade and fish. The fishery was about twenty miles below Rensselaerswyck. Growing tired of the life there, he told his "aunt" that he would like to return to their village, and she, who had grown very kind to him, gave him some food and set him on his way with some Indians. At the fort he heard of the determination of the Mohawks to do away with him. They considered him guilty of causing every misfortune that had befallen their warriors. The commandant of the fort urged him to escape on a vessel that was lying at anchor. He begged for time to consider the proposal. What he really desired to do was to think and pray over it, in order to do what would appear to be God's will. After concluding that to remain a prisoner now would mean speedy death, whereas escaping he might some day return and with his knowledge of the language and acquaintance with the tribes help them as a missionary, he decided to accept the commandant's offer.

It was not, however, so easy to get away. When the Indians found that he was aboard the vessel, they threatened reprisals. For peace's sake he came back to the post and there had to wait, hidden in a miserable barn, and comforted only by the genial Dutch minister, John Megapolensis, fully aware that braves had come down from Ossernenon to demand his return. The commandant was imperturbable. "The Frenchman you are seeking is under my protection. I cannot give him up. If I surrender him to you, I would be false to my own honor and humanity. . . . The course I have followed is sanctioned by all the Dutch; but to give you full satisfaction, here is gold for the ransom of your prisoner", offering him three hundred livres.

Jogues still had to wait some days hidden from the Iroquois, lying motionless behind some casks in the storehouse of the commissary. At last, by command of William Kieft, Governor of New Netherlands, he was taken aboard a vessel that was about to sail down the Hudson. With him was Domine Megapolensis, and some of the leading inhabitants, who, with their proverbial good nature, celebrated the deliverance of the captive, the Domine giving an entertainment to the crew in his honor, and the entire company joining in the festivities at an island in the river, which they wished to christen after Jogues, as we are told, "amid the noise of cannons and bottles".

Governor Kieft was particularly cordial to Jogues, inviting him, with the pastor of New Amsterdam, to his table, clothing him and providing for his passage home in a little vessel of fifty tons. Jogues was honored by Protestants and Catholics alike, though the latter were very few, among them a Portuguese woman, the wife of an ensign, and an Irishman who had come up from Virginia on hearing that there was a Catholic priest so near. Later Jogues will write his description

of Manhattan Island, under the name of New
Belgium, describing its rivers, Nassau to the north
and Maurice to the south (East River). Already
eighteen different languages were spoken there by
the inhabitants and almost as many religions were
practised, but the Calvinist was the only one recognized. The Church of the Fort, still functioning
under the name of the Collegiate Reformed Church,
was the central place of worship. Megapolensis
was soon to be made its fourth pastor.[84] The description of the island and its people is quite minute, in
Jogues' usual manner, and it is one of the earliest
written accounts of the Dutch settlements.

The missionary's adventures were not entirely
over. He narrates how, after an uncomfortable
voyage, with the ropes on deck for cabin and berth,
he reached England. After many mishaps he
reached the French coast on Christmas Eve, had
the consolation of worshipping at a village church
the next morning, and then went on to the nearest
Jesuit establishment, which was at Rennes, a journey of five days on horseback. One can imagine
his reception. His survival of so much ill-treatment, and his return to his native country excited
the keenest interest. At Paris, whither he went to
report to his Provincial, he was so much in demand,
as one who had suffered for Christ, that he longed
to escape from his notoriety and return to his mission. The queen, Anne of Austria, insisted on
seeing him and hearing his story. With mutilated

fingers he could not celebrate Mass, and this pained him grievously. It was not difficult to obtain from Pope Urban VIII special permission to offer the Holy Sacrifice, Urban remarking, "It would be unjust that a martyr for Christ should not drink the Blood of Christ".

Early in 1644 Jogues was at sea again, sailing for New France. On the voyage he had to quiet a mutiny of the sailors and calm them during a severe storm. On arriving, he was sent to Montreal, which had been founded on May 17th of the year he was taken captive. He immediately began to work among the Indians in that neighborhood, awaiting the time when he could safely venture back to Huronia. The journey thither had every year become more hazardous. The Iroquois warriors were everywhere along the route. In fact, instead of waiting for the Hurons to come down over their trails for trade, they had begun to enter the Huron territory and to destroy the villages. Even while Jogues was on his way back from France, Bressani and his companions and interpreters were seized and led in captivity to Ossernenon to undergo the same tortures as Jogues and Goupil. Bressani has left his narrative, "Brief Relation", as it is called, of his for months' imprisonment.[85] He also wrote an account of the torture and captivity of Jogues, which is an explanation of the Martyr's own narrative.[86]

Altogether unexpectedly, the Iroquois sent an embassy to Three Rivers to sue for peace. They arrived on July 5, 1644. The conferences were almost as long and as elaborate as peace conferences nowadays. They are described in the Relations of 1644.[87] Peace was not finally concluded until May, 1646. Jogues had been present at the conference. Knowing the Iroquois as he did, he perceived that the embassy did not represent the responsible captains of the tribe. No one was present from the principal village, Ossernenon. It was clear also that they wished to be at peace only with the French, not with the Hurons. However, it was considered proper to send an embassy from New France to meet the chiefs of the Iroquois at Ossernenon, and Jogues was selected as ambassador on this occasion, with John Bourdon, who had for ten years been active in the government of the colony.

Jogues knew full well what his mission was to be. Even the Indians about Three Rivers warned him to be cautious, advising him especially while on this errand not to mention religion, and even to leave aside his clerical robes, as the Mohawks hated the "black robe", as they called the missionary. Jerome Lalemant was also aware of the peril of the expedition. When referring to it in the Relation of 1646, he wrote: "When I speak of an Iroquois mission, it seems to me that I am talking of some dream; and yet it is a reality. With good

reason we have given it the name of 'Mission of
the Martyrs'; for, besides the cruelty which these
savages have already inflicted on some persons
devoted to the salvation of souls, besides the pains
and hardships which those appointed for this mission must encounter, we can say in truth, that it
has already been ensanguined with the blood of a
martyr, inasmuch as the Frenchman [René Goupil]
who was killed at the feet of Father Jogues lost
his life for having formed the sign of our Faith on
some little Iroquois children. If we are permitted
to conjecture in matters that seem highly probable,
we may believe that the designs we have formed
against the empire of Satan will not bear fruit till
they are irrigated with the blood of some other
martyrs".[88]

Jogues and Bourdon left Three Rivers May
16th, going down by the route of Lake Champlain
and Lake George. It was on this occasion he
christened it by its first name, Lake of the Holy
Sacrament. On the way he met Theresa Oiouhatan,
who had been captured with him in 1642 and given
in marriage to one of the captains. It consoled
him to find her so steadfast in her faith. On June
10th he met the sachems in general assembly. They
spent a week confirming their pact with New
France. On July 3rd Jogues was back in Quebec.

Determined to return to the Mohawks as missionary, Jogues had left at Ossernenon a box of
some pious articles. It was no slight relief not to

have to carry burdens over a trail that took so many days. This box was to be the cause of his death. The Mohawks had poor crops that year, and soon after Jogues' departure an epidemic broke out amongst them. They blamed the scarcity and the disease upon the box, which they superstitiously believed had a devil in it. When, therefore, they heard that Jogues was on his third visit to their villages, they waylaid him two days before his arrival, stripped and ill-treated him and John Lalande, his companion, with the one Huron guide that did not flee. His captors this time were members of the Bear Clan. The other clans did all they could to protect the prisoners, but to no purpose. They insisted that the fate of the prisoners should be decided in council, but the Bear family would not wait. Traitorously some of them invited Jogues to a meal on the evening of the 18th of October, and tomahawked him as he was entering the cabin. Cutting off his head, they put it on one of the palisade poles, facing the route over which he had come. The next day they tomahawked his companion, Lalande, and the faithful Huron, beheading them also, and throwing the bodies into the river.

The report of the martyrdoms reached Governor Montmagny from the Governor of New Netherlands in a letter dated November 14, 1646, enclosing the report of Labatie, secretary to the commandant at Fort Orange. The Indians carried to the

Dutch some of Jogues' possessions, his missal, ritual and cassock.

Lalemant's name for Ossernenon had been justified. It was now in reality the Mission of the Martyrs. Jogues, Apostle of the Iroquois, had been martyred by them there.

CHAPTER FOURTEEN
A Supreme Holocaust

Hurons becoming Christian—Example of devotion—Iroquois implacable—Daniel their victim, Martyr of Charity—Acts of the Martyrs—Brébeuf and Lalemant—An orgy of cruelties.

THE martyrdom of Jogues sealed the doom of the Hurons. Their only hope of peace was his success as missionary among their fierce enemies, the Iroquois. That would lead them to give up their habit of warfare and let the villagers to the north live quietly and prosper. No doubt Jogues was happy to throw himself into the breach with the hope of saving his beloved Huronia. It would appear, however, from a letter he wrote at the time to a Jesuit friend, Castillon in France, that he had a presentiment of what was to happen to him.

"My heart tells me that, if I have the blessing of being employed in this mission, 'I go not to return'; but I would be happy if Our Lord were willing to finish the sacrifice where He has begun it, and if the little blood which I have shed in that land were as the pledge of that which I would give him from all the veins of my body and my heart. In fine, that people 'is espoused to me in blood: I have espoused it in my blood'. Our Good Master Who has acquired it by His blood, opens to it, if He pleases, the door of His Gospel,—as also to

Gabriel Catement Soc. Jesu

four other nations, its allies, who are near to it. Adieu, my dear Father; entreat Him that He unite me inseparably to Himself."[89]

Since Jogues' departure from the Hurons in 1642, they began to embrace the Faith in increasing numbers. The number of missionaries employed and needed amongst them was now twenty-four. Daniel had returned in 1639, his seminary at Quebec for young Indian boys having proved a failure because the parents, who were still pagan, could not bear separation from their children for the sake of religious training which they could not appreciate. After a year at Ossossané, he spent eight years at St. John Baptist and the last year of his life at the second village of St. Joseph. Every "Relation" at this time reports not only a growth in Christianity, but remarkable instances of constancy and of singular virtue on the part of the new converts. Thus, when Brébeuf writes to his General in Rome, September 23, 1643, about the capture and torture of Jogues, he adds:

"From these things it is evident in what a very evil condition Canadian affairs are placed; but, on another side, these unhappy afflictions are by so much richer in heavenly gifts, as they are more lamentable. Not vice rules here, but virtue and piety; not only among ours, who everywhere show themselves men, and true sons of the Society; but also among our French and among the barbarians, — nor alone in the case of those barbarians who have already enrolled their names for the Faith, but also in the case of others who do not yet profess the Faith. For they scarcely practise their former superstitions; and we might hope, if we now enjoyed peace, to bring all, in a short time, to the Faith. . . ."[90]

Vimont soon after the capture of Jogues writes:

"As for our missions in the villages of the Hurons, we have continued them as usual. We were never so fortunate, nor ever so unfortunate — the capture of Father Jogues, of our Frenchmen, of our Christian Hurons, and of our catechumens, makes us realize our troubles; and what has occurred this year for the enlargement of the Faith publishes in the 'Relation' our blessedness. We are entering more and more into the possession of the goods which we come to buy in this end of the world at the price of our blood and of our lives: I see stronger tendencies than ever toward the total conversion of these peoples, whom we are attacking among the first, and whom we are undertaking to carry away, in order to serve as models and as examples to those who shall be subsequently converted. In a word, our little churches are continually increasing in number of persons, and in virtue; the affairs of Our Lord advance in proportion to the adversities which He sends us. Hardly could one find, hitherto, among our Christians two or three warriors; but, since the capture of that worthy neophyte, named Eustache, the most valiant of all the Hurons, we have counted in a single band as many as twenty-two believers,—all men of courage, and mostly captains or people of importance."[91]

Lalemant gives this description of one of the captains converted in the mission where Garnier and Le Moyne were at work:

"Father Charles Garnier and Father Simon Le Moyne have had charge of this mission. The number of Christians in it has increased in a marked degree. Among those who have received holy baptism, were three captains who are persons of consideration. The first is named Thomas Sondakwa. Some years ago he had already a desire to become a Christian; he never felt anything but love for us, and for the things of the Faith, and has always lived in a state of moral innocence and of goodness that made him loved by all. But as he saw that there was ill will against the Christians, and, moreover, as his office compelled him to uphold the superstitions of his country, which constitute the greater portion of their councils, his courage was not strong enough to choose altogether what he only partly desired. After the death of a friend of his, who was a Christian, and of whom I have spoken in one of the earlier chapters, God touched his heart more deeply. He commenced to receive instruction, he took pleasure in heavenly things, and resolved publicly to embrace the Faith. There-

13

upon the Devil frightens him in dreams. Sometimes he sees before his eyes a captain, who had
been one of his old friends, who comes back from
the other world, and reproaches him with his want
of affection in seeking thus to separate himself
forever from all those who had such affection for
him. On another occasion, he sees one whose face
he does not know, who puts in his mouth a morsel
that is to make him very fortunate; and indeed,
on awakening, he finds something on his tongue
that he cannot recogize, and that an infidel Huron
would have considered as a sign of good fortune,
and would have preserved as a gift from some
familiar demon. For it is thus that the demons
manifest themselves in these countries, under
assumed shapes,— sometimes an owl's claw, sometimes the skin of a hideous serpent, or similar things,
that bring with them good luck in fishing and hunting, in trading and gambling. Some of them are
even used as philters to attract love.

"Our catechumen was already too far advanced
in the sentiments of the Faith to be frightened by
such threats, or to yield to the Devil's promises. He
renounces all such hellish intercourse; he has
recourse to God; and after his baptism all these
phantoms disappear. He at once makes a public
profession of faith, refuses to attend the councils
when anything forbidden by the laws of God is
to be discussed, and wishes the entire country to
know that he prefers the duty of a Christian to any-

thing else. And the best part of all is, that in all this,— although he has manifested a truly heroic courage, by trampling on all human considerations, which prevail here not less than in France,— he nevertheless acts with such loving gentleness that those who are most hostile to the Faith can find nothing to blame in him. For this reason, this virtue of mildness is dear to his heart as the most powerful means of winning the infidels to Jesus Christ."[92]

In fact, the Hurons were gradually becoming Catholics, and as Brébeuf remarks, with a period of peace, the whole people would have been converted. The Iroquois, however, were unremitting in their hostilities to their former tribal associates. No longer content with attacking stray bands of Hurons on the trail, they began to enter and pillage their towns, sparing no one, neither women nor children. As early as 1642 they had destroyed a village on the outskirt, Kontarea. Their next attack was on the village of St. John Baptist and on July 4, 1648, they appeared at Teanaustayé just as Daniel had finished celebrating Mass. As Ragueneau narrates:

"Hardly had the Father ended Mass, and the Christians — who, according to their custom, had filled the church after the rising of the sun — were still continuing their devotions there, when the cry arose, 'To arms, and repel the enemy!'— who, having come unexpectedly, had made his approaches by night. Some hasten to the combat, others to flight: there is naught but alarm and terror everywhere. The Father, among the first to rush where he sees the danger greatest, encourages his people to a brave defense; and—as if he had seen paradise open for the Christians, and hell on the point of swallowing up all the infidels — he speaks to them in a tone so animated with the spirit which was possessing him, that, having made a breach in hearts which till then had been most rebellious, he gave them a Christian heart. The number of these proved to be so great that, unable to cope with it by baptizing them one after the other, he was constrained to dip his handkerchief in the water (which was all that necessity then offered him), in order to shed abroad as quickly as possible this grace on those poor savages, who cried mercy to him,— using the manner of baptizing which is called 'by aspersion'.

"Meanwhile, the enemy continued his attacks more furiously than ever; and, without doubt, it was a great blessing for the salvation of some that, at the moment of their death, baptism had given them the life of the soul, and put them in possession of an immortal life. When the Father saw that the Iroquois were becoming masters of the place, he,— instead of taking flight with those who were inviting him to escape in their company,— forgetting himself, remembered some old men and sick people, whom he had long ago prepared for

baptism. He goes through the cabins, and proceeds
to fill them with his zeal,— the infidels themselves
presenting their children in crowds, in order to
make Christians of them. Meanwhile the enemy,
already victorious, had set everything on fire, and
the blood of even the women and children irritated
their fury. The Father, wishing to die in his
church, finds it full of Christians, and of
catechumens who ask him for baptism. It was
indeed at that time that their faith animated their
prayers, and that their hearts could not belie their
tongues. He baptizes some, gives absolution to
others, and consoles them all with the sweetest
hope of the saints,— having hardly other words
on his lips than these: 'My brothers, to-day we
shall be in heaven.'

"The enemy was warned that the Christians had
betaken themselves, in very large number, into the
Church, and that it was the easiest and the richest
prey that he could have hoped for; he hastens
thither, with barbarous howls and stunning yells.
At the noise of these approaches, 'Flee, my brothers,'
said the Father to his new Christians, 'and bear
with you your Faith even to the last sigh. As for
me' (he added), 'I must face death here, as long
as I shall see here any soul to be gained for Heaven;
and, dying here to save you, my life is no longer
anything to me; we shall see one another again in
heaven.' At the same time, he goes out in the
direction whence come the enemy, who stop in

astonishment to see one man alone come to meet them, and even recoil backward, as if he bore upon his face the terrible and frightful appearance of a whole company. Finally,— having come to their senses a little, and being astonished at themselves, — they incite one another; they surround him on all sides, and cover him with arrows, until, having inflicted upon him a mortal wound from an arquebus shot,— which pierced him through and through, in the very middle of his breast,— he fell. Pronouncing the name of Jesus, he blessedly yielded up his soul to God,— truly as a good pastor, who exposes both his soul and his life for the salvation of his flock. It was then that those barbarians rushed upon him with as much rage as if he alone had been the object of their hatred. They strip him naked, they exercise upon him a thousand indignities; and there was hardly anyone who did not try to assume the glory of having given him the final blow, even on seeing him dead. The fire meanwhile was consuming the cabins; and when it had spread as far as the church, the Father was cast into it, at the height of the flames, which soon made of him a whole burnt-offering. Be this as it may, he could not have been more gloriously consumed than in the fires and lights of a *Chapelle ardente*."[93]

Ragueneau is the narrator of Daniel's martyrdom. He had every means of ascertaining the facts from those who witnessed them. Now that the era of martyrdom was in progress, the greatest care was taken to record in minute detail what each one suffered and in what dispositions he met death. Ragueneau's account of this is a veritable "Acts of the Martyrs." No one could know better than the missionary that the Iroquois were determined to exterminate the Hurons. Every priest on that mission knew what fate was awaiting him. The government at Quebec was powerless to protect its Huron wards. The certainty of death for the natives and for themselves only made the missionaries cling more devotedly to their posts. They would die one and all of them if need be, ministering salvation to the Christian Indians as true shepherds standing by their flocks.

Within a year, on March 16, 1649, the Iroquois attacked the village at which Brébeuf and Lalemant were stationed. They perpetrated unspeakable horrors upon the inhabitants, and their torture of the two missionaries was as atrocious as anything recorded in history. Ragueneau writes the following account of their martyrdom to Jerome Lalemant, then Superior at Quebec, in his "Relation of 1648–49":

"As early as the next morning, when we had assurance of the departure of the enemy,— having had, before that, certain news, through some escaped captives, of the deaths of Father Jean de Brébeuf and of Father Gabriel Lalemant,— we sent one of our Fathers and seven other Frenchmen to

seek their bodies at the place of their torture. They
found there a spectacle of horror,— the remains
of cruelty itself; or rather the relics of the love of
God, which alone triumphs in the death of martyrs.
I would gladly call them if I were allowed, by
that glorious name, not only because voluntarily,
for the love of God and for the salvation of their
neighbor, they exposed themselves to death, and to
a cruel death, if ever there was one in the world,—
for they could easily and without sin have put their
lives in safety, if they had not been filled with love
for God rather than for themselves. But much
rather would I thus call them, because, in addition
to the charitable dispositions which they have manifested on their side, hatred for the Faith and contempt for the name of God have been among the
most powerful incentives which have influenced the
mind of the barbarians to practise upon them as
many cruelties as ever the rage of tyrants obliged
the martyrs to endure, who, at the climax of their
tortures, have trimphed over both life and death.
As soon as they were taken captive, they were
stripped naked, and some of their nails were torn
out; and the welcome which they received upon
entering the village of St. Ignace was a hailstorm
of blows with sticks upon their shoulders, their
loins, their legs, their breasts, their bellies, and
their faces,— there being no part of their bodies
which did not then endure its torment. Father
Jean de Brébeuf, overwhelmed under the burden of

these blows, did not on that account lose care for his flock; seeing himself surrounded with Christians whom he had instructed, and who were in captivity with him, he said to them: 'My children, let us lift our eyes to heaven at the height of our afflictions; let us remember that God is the witness of our sufferings, and will soon be our exceeding great reward. Let us die in this faith; and let us hope from His goodness the fulfilment of His promises. I have more pity for you than for myself; but sustain with courage the few remaining torments. They will end with our lives; the glory which follows then will never have an end.' 'Echon', they said to him (this is the name which the Hurons gave the Father), 'our spirits will be in heaven when our bodies shall be suffering on earth. Pray to God for us, that He may show us mercy; we will invoke Him even until death.' Some Huron infidels — former captives of the Iroquois, naturalized among them, and former enemies of the Faith — were irritated by these words, and because our Fathers in their captivity had not their tongues captive. They cut off the hands of one, and pierced the other with sharp awls and iron points; they apply under their armpits and upon their loins hatchets heated red in the fire, and put a necklace of these about their necks in such a way that all the motions of their bodies gave them a new torture. For, if they attempted to lean forward, the red-hot hatchets which hung behind them burned the

[203]

shoulders everywhere; and if they thought to avoid that pain, bending back a little, their stomachs and breasts experienced a similar torment; if they stood upright, without leaning to one side or the other, these glowing hatchets, touching them alike on all sides, were a double torture to them. They put about them belts of bark, filled with pitch and resin, to which they set fire, which scorched the whole of their bodies. At the height of these torments Father Gabriel Lalemant lifted his eyes to heaven, clasping his hands from time to time, and uttering sighs to God, Whom he invoked to his aid. Father Jean de Brébeuf suffered like a rock, insensible to the fires and the flames, without uttering any cry, and keeping a profound silence, which astonished his executioners themselves; no doubt, his heart was then reposing in his God. Then, returning to himself, he preached to those infidels, and still more to many good Christian captives, who had compassion on him. Those butchers, indignant at his zeal, in order to hinder him from further speaking of God, girdled his mouth, cut off his nose, and tore off his lips; but his blood spoke much more loudly than his lips had done; and, his heart not being yet torn out, his tongue did not fail to render him service until the last sigh, for blessing God for these torments, and for animating the Christians more vigorously than he had ever done.

"In derision of holy baptism,— which these good Fathers had so charitably administered even at the breach, and in the hottest of the fight,— those wretches, enemies of the Faith, bethought themselves to baptize them with boiling water. Their bodies were entirely bathed with it, two or three times, and more, with biting gibes, which accompanied these torments. 'We baptize thee', said these wretches, 'to the end that thou mayst be blessed in heaven; for without proper baptism one cannot be saved.' Others added, mocking, 'We treat thee as a friend, since we shall be the cause of thy greatest happiness up in heaven; thank us for so many good offices,—for, the more thou sufferest, the more thy God will reward thee.'

"These were infidel Hurons, former captives of the Iroquois, and, of old, enemies of the Faith,— who having previously had sufficient instruction for their salvation, impiously abused it,— in reality, for the glory of the Fathers; but it is much to be feared that it was also for their own misfortune. The more these torments were augmented, the more the Fathers entreated God that their sins should not be the cause of the reprobation of these poor blind ones, whom they pardoned with all their heart. It is surely now that they say in repose, 'we have passed through fire and water, but Thou hast led us into a place of refreshment.' When they were fastened to the post where they suffered these torments, and where they were to die, they knelt down, they embraced it with joy, and kissed it piously as the object of their desires and their love,

[205]

and as a sure and final pledge of their salvation. They were there some time in prayers, and longer than those butchers were willing to permit them. They put out Father Gabriel Lalemant's eyes and applied burning coals in the hollows of the same. Their tortures were not of the same duration. Father Jean de Brébeuf was at the height of his torments at about three o'clock on the same day of the capture, the 16th day of March, and rendered up his soul about four o'clock in the evening. Father Gabriel Lalemant endured longer, from six o'clock in the evening until about nine o'clock the next morning, the 17th of March.

"Before their death, both their hearts were torn out, by means of an opening above the breast; and those barbarians inhumanly feasted thereon, drinking their blood quite warm, which they drew from its source with sacrilegious hands. While still quite full of life, pieces of flesh were removed from their thighs, from the calves of the legs, and from their arms,— which those executioners placed on coals to roast, and ate in their sight. They had slashed their bodies in various parts; and, in order to increase the feeling of pain, they had thrust into these wounds red hot hatchets. Father Jean de Brébeuf had had the skin which covered his skull torn away; they had cut off his feet and torn the flesh from his thighs, even to the bone, and had split, with the blow of a hatchet, one of his jaws in two. Father Gabriel Lalemant had received a

hatchet-blow on the left ear, which they had driven
into his brain, which appeared exposed; we saw no
part of his body, from the feet even to the head,
which had not been broiled, and in which he had
not been burned alive,— even the eyes, into which
those impious ones had thrust burning coals. They
had broiled their tongues, repeatedly putting into
their mouths flaming brands, and burning pieces of
bark,— not willing that they should invoke, in
dying, Him for whom they were suffering, and Who
could never die in their hearts. I have learned all
this from persons worthy of credence, who have
seen it, and reported it to me personally, and who
were then captives with them,— but who, having
been reserved to be put to death at another time,
found means to escape. But let us leave these
objects of horror, and these monsters of cruelty;
since one day all those parts will be endowed with
an immortal glory, the greatness of their torments
will be the measure of their happiness, and, from
now on, they live in the repose of the saints, and
will dwell in it forever.

"We buried these precious relics on Sunday, the
21st day of March, with so much consolation and
such tender feeling of devotion in all those who
were present at their obsequies, that I know none
who did not desire a similar death, rather than fear
it; and who did not regard himself as blest to stand
in a place where, it might be, two days thence, God
would accord him the grace of shedding both his

blood and his life on a like occasion. Not one of us could ever prevail upon himself to pray to God for them, as if they had had any need of it; but our spirits were at once directed toward heaven, where we doubted not that their souls were. Be this as it may, I entreat God that He fulfil upon us His will, even to death, as He has done in their persons."[94]

CHAPTER FIFTEEN
The Last of the Victims

The Hurons exterminated—Garnier at his post—A true Shepherd—His dying effort—A sublime burial-scene—Chabanel betrayed—His vow accepted.

IT would seem that after this triumph, as the Indians regarded an orgy of cruelties, they would have been sated with blood and that they would have been content with having broken the spirit of the Hurons and decimated their numbers. Still, it was not yet enough to satisfy their lust for blood. Before that year was ended, on December 7th, the Iroquois went even as far as the Tobacco Nation where Garnier had founded his Mission of the Apostles in 1641. The village was taken by surprise. It is Ragueneau again who tells of the destruction wrought by this implacable enemy and of the death of the missionaries Garnier and Chabanel:

"In the mountains, the people of which we name the Tobacco Nation, we have had, for some years past, two missions; in each were two of our Fathers. The one nearest to the enemy was that which bore the name of Saint Jean; its principal village, called by the same name, contained about five or six hundred families. It was a field watered by the sweat of one of the most excellent missionaries who had

dwelt in these regions, Father Charles Garnier,—
who was also to water it with his blood, since there
both he and his flock have met death, he himself
leading them even unto paradise. The day approach-
ing in which God would make a church triumphant
of that which, up to that time, had always been in
warfare, and which could bear the name of a
church truly suffering, we received intelligence of it,
toward the close of the month of November, from
two Christian Hurons, escaped from a band of
about three hundred Iroquois, who told us that
the enemy was still irresolute as to what measures
he would take,— whether against the Tobacco
Nation, or against the island on which we were.
Thereupon, we kept ourselves in a state of defense,
and detained our Hurons, who had purposed taking the field to meet that enemy. At the same
time, we caused the tidings to be speedily conveyed
to the people of the Tobacco Nation, who received
it with joy, regarding that hostile band as already
conquered, and as occasion for their triumph. They
resolutely awaited them for some days; then, weary-
ing because victory was so slowly coming to them,
they desired to go to meet it,— at least, the inhabitants of the village of Saint Jean, men of enterprise
and valor. They hastened their attack, fearing lest
the Iroquois should escape them, and desiring to
surprise the latter while they were still on the road.
They set out on the fifth day of the month of
December, directing their route toward the place

where the enemy was expected. But the latter, having taken a roundabout way, was not met; and, to crown our misfortunes, the enemy, as they approached the village, seized upon a man and woman who had just come out of it. They learned from these two captives the condition of the place, and ascertained that it was destitute of the better part of its people. Losing no time, they quickened their pace that they might lay waste everything, opportunity so greatly favoring them.

"It was on the seventh day of the month of last December, in the year 1649, toward three o'clock in the afternoon, that this band of Iroquois appeared at the gates of the village, spreading immediate dismay, and striking terror into all those poor people,—bereft of their strength, and finding themselves vanquished, when they thought to be themselves the conquerors. Some took to flight; others were slain on the spot. To many, the flames, which were already consuming some of their cabins, gave the first intelligence of the disaster. Many were taken prisoners; but the victorious enemy, fearing the return of the warriors who had gone to meet them, hastened their retreat so precipitately, that they put to death all the old men and children, and all whom they deemed unable to keep up with them in their flight. It was a scene of incredible cruelty. The enemy snatched from a mother her infants, that they might be thrown into the fire; other children beheld their mothers beaten to death at their feet, or groaning in the flames,— permission, in either case, being denied them to show the least compassion. It was a crime to shed a tear, these barbarians demanding that their prisoners should go into captivity as if they were marching to their triumph. A poor Christian mother, who wept for the death of her infant, was killed on the spot, because she still loved, and could not stifle soon enough her natural feelings.

"Father Charles Garnier was, at that time, the only one of our fathers in that mission. When the enemy appeared, he was just then occupied with instructing the people in the cabins which he was visiting. At the noise of the alarm, he went out, going straight to the church, where he found some Christians. 'We are dead men, my brothers', he said to them. 'Pray to God, and flee by whatever way you may be able to escape. Bear about with you your Faith through what of life remains; and may death find you with God in mind'. He gave them his blessing, then left hurriedly, to go to the help of souls. A prey to despair, not one dreamed of defence. Several found a favorable exit for their flight; they implored the Father to flee with them, but the bonds of charity restrained him. All unmindful of himself, he thought only of the salvation of his neighbor. Borne on by his zeal, he hastened everywhere,—either to give absolution to the Christians whom he met, or to seek, in the burning cabins, the children, the sick, or the catechumens, over whom, in the midst of the flames, he poured the waters of holy baptism, his own heart burning with no other fire than the love of God. It was while thus engaged in holy work that he was encountered by the death which he had looked in the face without fearing it, or receding from it a single step. A bullet from a musket struck him, penetrating a little below the breast; another, from the same volley, tore open his stomach, lodging in the thigh, and bringing him to the ground. His courage, however, was unabated. The barbarian who had fired the shot stripped off his cassock, and left him, weltering in his blood, to pursue the other fugitives.

"This good Father, a very short time after, was seen to clasp his hands, offering some prayer; then, looking about him, he perceived, at a distance of ten or twelve paces, a poor dying man,—who, like himself, had received the stroke of death, but had still some remains of life. Love of God, and zeal for souls, were even stronger than death. Murmuring a few words of prayer, he struggled to his knees, and, rising with difficulty, dragged himself as best he might toward the sufferer, in order to assist him in dying well. He had made but three or four steps, when he fell again, somewhat heavily. Raising himself for the second time, he got, once more, upon his knees and strove to continue on his way; but his body, drained of its blood, which was flowing in abundance from his wounds, had not the strength of his courage. For the third time he fell, having proceeded but five or six steps. Further than this, we have not been able to ascertain what he accomplished,—the good Christian woman who faithfully related all this to us having seen no more of him, being herself overtaken by an Iroquois, who struck her on the head with a war-hatchet, felling her upon the spot, though she afterwards escaped. The Father, shortly after, received from a hatchet two blows upon the temples, one on either side, which penetrated to the brain. To him it was the recompense for all past services, the richest he had hoped for from God's goodness. His body was stripped, and left, entirely naked, where it lay.

"Two of our Fathers, who were in the nearest neighboring mission, received a remnant of these poor fugitive Christians, who arrived all out of breath, many of them all covered with their own blood. The night was one of continual alarm, owing to the fear, which had seized all, of a similar misfortune. Toward the break of day, it was ascertained from certain spies that the enemy had retired. The two Fathers at once set out, that they might themselves look upon a spectacle most sad indeed, but nevertheless acceptable to God. They found only dead bodies heaped together, and the remains of poor Christians,—some who were almost consumed in the pitiable remains of the still burning village; others deluged with their own blood; and a few who yet showed some signs of life, but were all covered with wounds,—looking only for death, and blessing God in their wretchedness. At length, in the midst of that desolated village they descried the body they had come to seek; but so little cognizable was it, being completely covered with its blood, and the ashes of the fire, that they passed it by. Some Christian savages, however, recognized their Father, who had died for love of them. They buried him in the same spot on which their church had stood, although there remained no longer any vestige of it, the fire having consumed all. The poverty of that burial was sublime, and its sanctity no less so. The two good Fathers divested themselves of part of their apparel, to cover therewith the dead; they could do no more, unless it were to return entirely unclothed. It was truly a rich treasure to deposit in so desolate a spot, the body of so noble a servant of God; but that great God will surely find a way to reunite us all in Heaven, since it is for His sake alone that we are thus scattered, both during life and after death".[95] Here is the sixth victim whom God has taken to himself from those of our Society whom He had called to this Mission of the Hurons,—there having been, as yet, not one of us who has died there without shedding his blood, and consummating the sacrifice in its entirety.

"Father Noel Chabanel was the missionary companion of Father Charles Garnier; and when the village of Saint Jean was taken by the Iroquois, there were but two days in which they were separated, in accordance with the orders which they had received,—our Fathers and I having thought it wiser not to keep two missionaries exposed to danger; considering, besides, that the famine in that quarter was so severe that sufficient food for both could not be obtained. But it was not God's will that, having lived and been yoked together in the same mission, they should be separated in death. This good Father, then, returning whither obedience recalled him, had passed through the mission of Saint Mathias, where were two other of our Fathers, and had left them on the morning of the seventh day of December. Having travelled six long leagues over a most difficult road, he found himself overtaken by night in the thick of the forest, being in the company of seven or eight Christian Hurons. His men were resting, and asleep; he only was watching, and in prayer. Toward midnight, he heard a noise, accompanied with cries,—partly of a victorious hostile force who occupied that road; partly, also of captives ,taken that very day in the village of Saint Jean, who were singing, as was their custom, their war-song. On hearing the noise, the Father awoke his men, who fled at once into the forest, and eventually saved themselves,—scattering, some here, some there; and taking their route toward the very place from which the enemy had come out, though a little at one side of it. These

Christians, escaped from the peril, arrived at the Tobacco Nation, and reported that the Father had gone some little way with them, intending to follow them; but that, becoming exhausted, he had fallen on his knees, saying to them, 'It matters not that I die; this life is a very small consideration; of the blessedness of Paradise, the Iroquois can never rob me'. At daybreak, the Father, having altered his route, desirous of coming to the island where we were, found himself checked at the bank of a river, which crossed his path. A Huron reported the circumstance, adding that he had passed him, in his canoe, on this side of the stream; and that, to render his flight more easy, the Father had disburdened himself of his hat, and of a bag that contained his writings; also of a blanket, which our missionaries use as robe and cloak, as mattress and cushion, for a bed, and for every other convenience,—even for a dwelling-place, when in the open country, and when they have, for the time, no other shelter. Since then, we have been unable to learn any other news of the Father."

In the narrative Ragueneau states that the manner of his death was uncertain, but in a note appended to the Memoir of 1652 he states that it was learned from most trustworthy witnesses; a Huron apostate Louis Honareenhax had admitted he had killed Chabanel through hatred of the Faith.[96]

"Father Noel Chabanel had come to us from the
Province of Toulouse, in the year 1643, having
been received into our Society as early as the year
1630, when he was only seventeen years of age.
God had given him a strong vocation for these
countries; but, once here, he had much to contend
with; for, even after three, four, and five years
of effort to learn the language of the savages, he
found his progress so slight, that hardly could he
make himself understood even in the most ordinary
matters. This was no little mortification to a man
who burned with desire for the conversion of the
savages, who in other ways was deficient neither in
memory nor mind, and who had made this manifest
enough by having for some years successfully taught
rhetoric in France. In consequence of this, the
temper of his mind was so opposed to the ways and
manners of the savages, that he saw in them scarce
anything that pleased him; the sight of them, their
talk, and all that concerned them, he found irksome.
He could not accustom himself to the food of the
country; and residence in the missions did such
violence to his entire nature that he encountered
therein extraordinary hardships, without any consolation,—at least, of the character that we call
sensible. There, one must always sleep on the bare
ground, and live from morning to night in a little
hell of smoke; in a place where often, of a morning,
one finds himself covered with the snows that drift
on all sides into the cabin of the savages; where

vermin abound; where the senses, each and all, are tormented both night and day. One never has anything but water to quench his thirst; while the best food usually eaten there is only a paste made with meal of Indian corn boiled in water. One must work there incessantly, though always so poorly nourished; never have one moment in the day in which to retire to any spot that is not public; have no other room, no other apartment, no other closet, in which to prosecute his studies. One has not even any other light than that of a smoky fire,—surrounded, at the same time, by ten or fifteen persons, and children of all ages, who scream, weep, and wrangle; who are busied about their cooking, their meals, their work, about everything, in a word, that is done in a house. When God, besides all this, withdraws His sensible graces, and hides Himself from a person who longs only for him,—when He leaves him a prey to sorrow, to disgusts, and repugnances of nature,—these are trials that are not within the compass of ordinary virtue; and the love of God must be strong in a heart, if it is not to be stifled by them. Join to these the continual sight of dangers, in which one finds himself at every moment, of attack by a savage enemy who often will subject you to the sufferings of a thousand deaths, ere death itself ensues; who uses only fire, and flames, and unheard-of cruelties. Doubtless a courage is needed worthy of the children of God,

[219]

15

if one is not to lose heart in the midst of such abandonment.

"It has been in this abandonment that God has willed to put to the test, for five or six years, the fidelity of this good Father; but assuredly the Devil never having got the better of him upon that account, although he represented to him every day that, by returning to France, he would find there the joy, repose, and comfort which during all his past life he had received; that there he would not lack employment better suited to his disposition, employment in which so many saintly souls nobly practise the virtue of charity in a zeal for souls, and expend their lives for the salvation of their fellow-men. Never, for all that, would he break away from the Cross on which God had placed him; never did he ask that he might come down from it. On the contrary, in order to bind himself to it more inviolably, he obliged himself, by a vow, to remain there till death, so that he might die upon the Cross. These are the terms of the vow, as he conceived it, and its very words:

" 'Jesus Christ, my Savior, why by a wonderful dispensation of your paternal providence have willed that I, though altogether unworthy, should be a coadjutor of the holy Apostles in this vineyard of the Hurons; impelled by the desire of ministering to the purpose which Your holy Spirit hath respecting me, that I should help forward the conversion to the faith of the barbarians of this Huron country: I, Noel Chabanel,—being in the presence of the most holy Sacrament of Your Body and Your Precious Blood, which is the tabernacle of God among men,—make a vow of perpetual stability in this Mission of the Hurons; understanding all things as the superiors of the Society expound them, and as they choose to dispose of me. I conjure You, therefore, O my Savior, to be pleased to receive me as a perpetual servant of this Mission, and to make me worthy of so lofty a ministry. Amen.' "[97]

CHAPTER SIXTEEN
Fruits of Martyrdom

An exterminated people—The Missions not a failure—Virtues
of the Missionaries—Their memory in veneration—Influence
after death—Monuments in their honor—Protestant devotion—
General Clark and Auriesville, site of Jogues' death—The long
memory of the Church.

THE Hurons were an exterminated people.
Gradually the missionaries gathered the
remnants of their race in reservations about Quebec.
In one sense the missions in Huronia and the sur-
rounding country were a failure. The Iroquois
mercilessly destroyed the Neutrals and the Eries.
They harassed the Algonquins and the Ottawas,
while all this time some of their warriors were
fighting with the Mohicans to the south and the
Illinois and Cherokees to the west.

Apparently the time, labor, self-sacrifice, suffering and even the death of the martyred priests and
their two companions had gone for naught. They,
of course, and their fellow-missionaries thought
otherwise. It was enough for the martyrs that for
them the mission was an occasion of sacrifice. It
had civilized and christianized many souls. It had
even cultivated many of them to extraordinary
devotion, Stephen Totiri, for instance, Teresa Oiou-
haton, Theondechoren, Tsondatsaa, Ahasistari, as
it would later, Tekakwitha, Lily of the Mohawks.
The martyrdoms themselves aroused a new fervor
both in New and Old France. They were an

inspiration to the missionaries who were already working in the field, and to the three hundred and twenty others of the Jesuits alone, who were to work at saving the remnant of it, developing the vast continent beyond the gate at Sault Ste. Marie, which Jogues had happily opened.

The lay auxiliaries of the missionaries would grow in number, whilst their two champions were dying for the Faith, from six to twenty-three. No sooner would word of the death of Goupil, "gallant surgeon", as Vimont called him, reach Jogues' native city, than another well known young surgeon at Orleans would gallantly offer to take his place.[98]

Could the humility of the Martyrs have allowed them to dream of the glorious outcome of their sacrifice, they would have entered into their bliss before consummating their ordeal. They knew their blood would not be an unfruitful seed, but they could never have imagined how soon their successors, Le Moyne and Le Mercier, Dablon and Lamberville, Fremin and Bruyas, would be down among their very executioners in their Mohawk Valley strongholds, "taking captive their fierce conquerors" in the toils of the Faith in Christ. Much less could they have had the vision of Ménard, Allouez, Druillettes, and finally Marquette pushing their way into the lakes, valleys and rivers of the great west and south, developing the new French civilization which Le Jeune had designed, and visiting and Christianizing members of "every tribe, and tongue, and people, and nation",[99] among the Indians. This vision, as well as the vision of a great new people in Canada, growing out of the handful of colonists who were there when they died, was reserved for them as part of their reward where they rest from their labors in the vision of God who hath accomplished all this with their aid as His instruments. In it all endures, and will endure for eternity, not only the memory of what they did, but the fruit of it in the countless generations that hold them in honor.

Not only among the three million Canadians of French origin, who are signed and sealed with the tradition that the Martyrs and their associates planted in them; not only among the Catholic people in this part of North America and all the world over, but among Protestants also, and men and women of no faith, is the memory of Jogues, Brébeuf and their companions alive today and a source of inspiration to nobler ideals and appreciation of real religious faith. The missions in Huronia were far from being a failure.

After reading Brébeuf's remarkable self-revelation in his charge to missionary candidates, and Jogues' pathetic confession during his captivity, it is needless to dwell upon their extraordinary virtues. All the missionaries who came to Canada were men of superior training and character. Le Jeune, Ragueneau, Vimont, Charles and Jerome Lalemant, Le Moyne, towering as they are in moral stature, are only types of the rank and file, over three hundred in number, who served on these missions for one hundred and forty years. Seven others, besides the martyrs mentioned in these pages, died at the hands of the Iroquois, and two, Rasle and Delmas besides, died for religion. Three were imprisoned, and fifteen perished by shipwreck, drowning and attending the plague-stricken. They were all men of refinement and knowledge. They knew beforehand all the hardships, the perils and the risk of death. Once at their post, they clung to it as if their lot was an enviable one. Their faith in God, their hope in His goodness, their love of Him and of souls, were extraordinary. They were men of singular prudence and fortitude, necessarily most abstemious of habit, with a fine sense of justice which led them to see, even in their enemies, merits and rights which they felt under obligation to respect. In all these virtues the eight Martyrs excelled. Garnier considered it a favor from Almighty God that he was permitted to serve on such a mission, as did Jogues. Daniel felt that he owed it to his Indians not only to instruct them but to lead them along the way of Christian perfection. Lalemant and Chabanel had little time on the missions to manifest their special virtues, but Lalemant had shown his by his many years of effort to be appointed missionary before he was finally chosen. Chabanel's vow is sufficient evidence of his heroism. They were all prayerful men, the lay auxiliaries as well as the priests, and they not only faced the likelihood of martyrdom with composure, but even desired it.

It is no wonder, therefore, that they have been held in veneration by all who knew the story of the birth of the New World. Immediately after the death of Garnier and Chabanel, the Archbishop of Rouen, who at that time claimed jurisdiction over the Canadian Missions, instituted an inquiry into their virtues and the heroic manner of their death for religion. Father Paul Ragueneau, then Superior of the Missions, collected from different sources his famous 'Memoir' concerning the virtues of these martyrs, and of others also of the missionaries who had died in the discharge of their duties. It was to be used as a plea for their beatification. So high was the regard of the faithful both in New and Old France for the saintliness of these men, that many were moved to invoke their intercession with Almighty God for needed temporal and spiritual favors. Remarkable answers to such prayers were occasionally recorded, as for instance, the cure ot Marie Brevost at Poitiers, attributed to the intercession of Jogues soon after his death, and many similar remarkable cures since then, notably that of a Sister of Mercy in Buffalo, November 17, 1906, and of numerous others which have been recorded in the 'Pilgrim of Our Lady of Martyrs' since 1886.[100] In the annals of the Hospital Sisters at Quebec is an account of one of their most distinguished members who with her sister was desirous of leaving France for the Canadian Mission. They could not prevail upon their father to give his consent, but he changed his mind overnight after reading the narrative of Jogues' sufferings and death. Similar remarkable favors are believed to have been received through the intercession of Brébeuf and his companions. One of these, the relief of a woman from demoniac possession, is recorded in the archives of the Diocese of Quebec under date of August 9, 1663. Others are mentioned in the 'Relations.'[101] Indeed, the 'Relations' contain numerous proofs of the veneration of these Martyrs and of the belief in their power of intercession.

Thus, in reporting one hundred and fifty-one baptisms among the Mohawks during the years 1668 and 1669, the writer adds: "The birth of this flourishing Church is due, next to God, to the death and the blood of the Reverend Father Jogues. He poured out his blood on the same spot where this new Christianity is beginning to be born; and we seem to be able in our day to verify, in his person, those beautiful words of Tertullian,—that 'the blood of the Martyrs is the seed of the Christians'."[102] Again in the 'Relation' for 1648–1649, it is stated:

"From the death of Father Antoine Daniel, which occurred July Fourth of last year, 1648, up to that of Father Jean de Brébeuf and of Father Gabriel Lalemant, who were burned and eaten on the 16th and 17th of the month of March in the present year, 1649, we baptized more than thirteen hundred persons; and, from the latter murders up to the month of August, we baptized more than fourteen hundred. Thus, the Christian Church was increased by more than two thousand seven hundred souls in thirteen months, without counting those baptized at the Breach (i.e., the storming of the Huron villages), and those who were made Christians in other places. So true are those words, *Sanguis Martyrum semen est Christianorum,*—'The blood of the Martyrs', if they may be so named, 'is the seed and germ of the Christians'."[103]

From the Mohawk Mission in 1670 Millet, after telling how he had made a difficult conversion through the help of Jogues, adds: "During the year that I have spent here, I have baptized nearly fifty persons, nine or ten of whom died happily after baptism; three or four have escaped me—two children and an old woman who, notwithstanding my efforts, died without baptism. My heart bleeds for them, and I am inconsolable."[104]

Le Jeune will account for the grace of baptism to a dying Iroquois by the fact that he had been one of those who attacked the village where Brébeuf and Lalemant died and had actually for a time saved the two Fathers from the fury of their captors. One of the torturers of these two missionaries died a Christian, as also did the man who tomahawked Jogues. Chauchetière in 1672 says that of the Indians then living at La Prairie the Mohawks took the first rank as Christians, and he ascribes this to the death of Jogues and also of Brébeuf who has been killed by members of that tribe.

Evidences of veneration for these Martyrs are found in many places. Their names are favorite ones for many Catholic organizations. Near the site of Ihonatiria at Penetanguishene is a church erected to their memory. At Waubashene on the site of one of the villages is a place of pilgrimage and a House of Retreats. Brébeuf's relics are encased in a silver bust of natural size presented to his fellow Jesuits by his family, and, from 1802 until now in possession of the Hotel Dieu at Quebec. On one of the family tombs, at Venoix near Caen in France, is inscribed a record of his martyrdom, and there is a memorial window of him in the Church of St. Martin (Anglican) at Brighton, England.

There are memorials of Jogues at Westport, on Lake Champlain, where he was tortured on the way down to the Mohawk settlement. There is an oratory dedicated to him at the home of the Paulist Fathers on Lake George. One of the principal statues at Dunwoodie Seminary is of Jogues. His principal monument is at Auriesville, the present name of the site of the village of Ossernenon where he was tortured and kept as a slave. During the summer of every year since 1884 there have been large pilgrimages from the cities along the Valley and occasionally from more distant centres, the pilgrims often exceeding five thousand in number, all of them devoutly convinced that Jogues is among the Blessed in heaven and more powerful now to intercede with Almighty God than when he was on earth.

The site at Auriesville was fixed by the late General John D. Clark of Auburn, New York, with the aid of the historian, Gilmary Shea, Reverend Clarence Walworth of Albany, and others who were expert in the study of Indian remains and village sites. Fortunately, Jogues' description of the place and its surroundings had been so detailed, and his estimate of distances so precise, that there can be no doubt about the General's conclusions. The pains which this devoted Protestant took to determine the actual site of the Mohawk village are only one instance of what has been done for Jogues by men who, like Governor Kieft of New Amsterdam, now New York, Commandant of Fort Orange, now Albany, Arendt van Corlaer, and the others who sought to rescue him, though not of his Faith, venerated him even in life for his Christian heroism. Since the Canadian Government published its edition of the 'Jesuit Relation' in 1858, there has been a 'cloud of testimony' from writers of every creed, Parkman, Bancroft, Kip, Thwaites, Finley, to speak only of those who are of our own country, all testifying with affection to the supreme devotion of Jogues and of his companions to the cause of religion and civilization.

The reader may imagine the impressions of the writer of this book on receiving in 1904 the following letter from General Clark:

"It will give me great pleasure to aid in any manner possible in the Beatification of Father Jogues and his companions. The same charges that were made against Jogues were made against the Huron missionaries, against Brébeuf and Chaumont when they visited the Neutrals in 1640, and against the missionaries who visited the Tobacco Nation. They were held responsible for all the public and private calamities to which the people had been subject. The box that Jogues left among the Mohawks is a fine example of the ridiculous and absurd suspicions that the enemies of the French and of the Faith had succeeded in spreading everywhere, and naturally a spirit of vengeance was aroused against the man who was looked upon as the author of all their woes. I say enemies of the Faith, because there can be no question in regard to this matter. It was 'the doctrine' that caused their death by charms and spells, it was this that caused the destruction of their grain and produced contagious diseases."

Six years before, this same devout Indian antiquarian had written: "My philological researches located the castle sites at the mouth of the river and between the two rivers. My mythological researches reveal why Jogues was condemned to death. The Turtle and Wolf clans were brothers and formed one side of the Council, the 'peace' side. The Bear and Beavers were brothers and constituted the 'war' side of the Council. The peace side made every effort to save his life, but their efforts could not prevail against those favoring the bloody sacrifice. Agreskoui, whom Jogues has offended, must be appeased by blood. He was sacrificed to appease the Sun God, Agreskoui, or God of War."

With sentiments like that prevailing among Christian people everywhere, it is not surprising that the Catholic hierarchy of the United States in 1884 authorized a formal preliminary inquiry into the lives and deaths of these servants of God with a view to ascertaining whether the result would justify a petition to the Holy See for opening the Apostolic process necessary for their beatification. The wonder everywhere is that this had not been done long before. Although an inquiry was instituted after the death of the Martyrs, many things conspired to prevent its completion— a change in the Episcopal jurisdiction of Canada; the unsettled condition of the missions there; the suppression of the Society of Jesus to which the missionaries belonged; the disturbance caused by the French Revolution; the interval between the suppression and the restoration of the Jesuits in Canada in 1842; the time it took to discover all the 'Relations' of the Jesuits and make them available as testimony for the Martyrs; and, finally, the patience and time required for the process of beatification itself. Needless to say, that in the course of this process, an important factor in helping the Commission which conducted it to a conclusion in favor of the beatification of these Martyrs, was the testimony of so many who are not of the Catholic faith and who yet had publicly testified in their writings to their veneration for these noble men.

The Church of Christ has a long memory. It ranges over the past, and views in detail its conflicts and its conquests, its apparent failures and its glorious triumphs. The heroes who have achieved these triumphs are never forgotten. Out of annals of remote times and obscure places it selects those who best exemplified in their members as well as in their spirit, their Divine exemplar Christ. These, already immortal in supernal bliss, it endows with an immortality among the faithful still striving toward that goal. Our land is fortunate that the first to be so favored were so heroic as to surpass even the most extravagant and mythical heroes of other lands; fortunate also in that their holiness was such as to inspire veneration and imitation, to some extent, by all who value what is noblest in human life. The achievements in science, literature, art and politics of the men who lived in the half-century during which our Martyrs lived and died, still exert their influence and excite our admiration. Excellent as these achievements were, they are not to be compared with the heroic accomplishments of these Martyrs. It is the difference between mental and moral grandeur. As we benefit by the science, art and literature, the mental genius of that day, may we not hope to benefit also by its examples of holiness, the moral and supernatural genius of these men. The blood of these Martyrs was to be Christian seed, not for races that are now extinct, but for our own that is only in the making. Why should it not so fructify that men born and things done in our day be as immortal as the men and things of the half-century which produced our Martyrs?

Sunday, June 21st, has been chosen for the formal declaration by the Holy See that Isaac Jogues, Jean de Brebeuf, Noel Chabanel, Anthony Daniel, Charles Garnier, Gabriel Lalemant, Rene Goupil and John Lalande died for the Faith and therefore deserve to be called Martyrs. They are consequently entitled to public veneration. It was behooves all who believe in the intercession of the Blessed in heaven to invoke their aid for favors, temporal or spiritual, that are beyond the ordinary powers of nature, for the miracles which will prove that the Church has been justified in declaring them Blessed, and that there is every reason for declaring them Saints as the final step towards their glorification.

REFERENCES

IN quoting the translation of the Relations in Thwaites' collection of "The Jesuit Relations and Allied Documents", we have omitted the page references to the original editions of the Relations. We have not followed the capitalization, as the translators did in imitation of the archaic French custom.

In the reference to Jogues' letter to his Provincial: — those who are familiar with Biblical language will recognize throughout this quotation allusions, phrases and often complete texts. The translators of the Thwaites collection left these in their Latin expression; we have put them into English.

REF.
No.

1. Bros, L'Ethnologie Religieuse, 126.
2. Fraser, Fifteenth Report of the Bureau of Archives for the Province of Ontario, 1818–19; Rev. Pierre Potier's collection.
3. De Vere, Essays Chiefly on Poetry, II, 240.
4. Bancroft, History of the U. S., III, 120.
5. MS. Vie du R. P. Isaac Jogues, 1792, p. 5.
6. Holweck, A Biographical Dictionary of the Saints.
7. Hanotaux, Histoire de la Nation Française, VI; Histoire religieuse, by Goyau, p. 384.
8. Rochemonteix, II, 326.
9. Harris, Missions of Western Canada, p. 212.
10. Ranke, History of the Popes, tr. Kelly (London, 1843), IV, 188.
11. Schwickerath, Jesuit Education, 182, 484.
12. Rame, Documents inédits sur Jacques Cartier au Canada, pp. 12–17 (Paris, 1868), quoted by Goyau, Les origines religeuses du Canada, CI, 3.
13. Goyau, ibid.

Ref.
No.

14. Ferland, Histoire du Canada, p. 5.
16. Ibid., p. 14.
17. Perrault, Relation, 1634–36, in Thwaites, Jesuit Relations, VIII, 157.
18. Rochemonteix, Les Jésuites et la nouvelle France, I, 66.
19. Factum des procès entre Jean de Biencourt et les Pères Biard et Massé, Jésuites; attributed to Lescarbot; republished, Paris, 1887.
20. Letter to the General of the Society of Jesus, Thwaites, II, 73.
21. Thwaites, Jesuit Relations, IV, 255–260, for valuable and judicious notes on this subject.
22. Le Jeune, Relation, 1634, Thwaites, VII, 35.
23. Brébeuf to Le Jeune, in Thwaites, Jesuit Relations, 1636, VIII, 75–81.
24. Thwaites, Jesuit Relations 1635, 1636, VIII, 69–155; X, 125.
25. Thwaites, Jesuit Relations, X, 45.
26. Martin, Le P. Jean de Brébeuf, sa vie, ses travaux, son martyre (Paris, 1877), 75.
27. Kingsford, Canada, I, 149.
28. Rochemonteix, Les Jésuites de la nouvelle France, I, 190, sqq.
29. Goyau, Les origines religieuses du Canada, p. 70.
30. Thwaites, Jesuit Relations, 1634, VIII, 9.
31. Wynne, The Pilgrim of Our Lady of Martyrs, 1897, pp. 81, 121, 152.
32. Life and Letters of St. Francis Xavier, II, p. 167.
33. Parkman, The Jesuits in North America, preface, vi.
34. Bancroft, History of the U. S., III, chap. xx, 122.
35. Field, Indian Bibliography.
36. Thwaites, Jesuit Relations, I, 38–40.
37. Finley, The French in the Heart of America, p. 30.
38. Lafitau, Les Moeurs des Sauvages.
39. Thwaites, Jesuit Relations, I, pp. 41–44.
40. Thwaites, Jesuit Relations, 1682, V, 42.
41. Thwaites, Jesuit Relations, VIII, 308, note.
42. Thwaites, Jesuit Relations, 1637, XI, 81.
43. Brébeuf's Report to Le Jeune, in Thwaites, Jesuit Relations, 1636, VIII, 81.
44. Thwaites, Jesuit Relations, 1635, VIII, 105–9.
45. Thwaites, Jesuit Relations, VIII, 133.
46. Thwaites, Jesuit Relations, VIII, 143.
47. Thwaites, Jesuit Relations, XII, 61 sqq.

REF.
No.

48. Thwaites, Jesuit Relations, X, 89–111.
49. Martin-Shea, Life of Isaac Jogues, p. 24.
50. Ibid., Idem, p. 29.
51. Ibid., Idem, p. 28.
52. Thwaites, Jesuit Relations, L636, IX, 279.
53. Martin-Shea, Life of Isaac Jogues, p. 35.
54. Ibid., Idem, p. 37.
55. Thwaites, Jesuit Relations, XV, 165.
56. Ibid., Idem, XVII, 13.
57. Ibid., Idem, X, 53.
58. Ibid., Idem, XI, 15.
59. Martin-Shea, Life of Isaac Jogues, p. 45.
60. Ibid., Idem, p. 49.
61. Ibid., Idem, p. 50.
62. Thwaites, Jesuit Relations, XV, 61.
63. Ibid., Idem, XV, 95.
64. Ibid., Idem, XIX, 227.
65. Thwaites, Jesuit Relations, XXV, 75–79.
66. Ibid., Idem, LXXI, 393.
67. Ibid., Idem, LXXI, 393.
68. Ibid., Idem, XVIII, 23.
69. Ibid., Idem, XX, 43.
70. Ibid., Idem, XXIII, 225.
71. Ibid., Idem, XVIII, 237.
72. Ibid., Idem, XXXIV, 163.
73. Ibid., Idem, XXI, 187.
74. Newman, Parochial and Plain Sermons, IV, 258.
75. Brucker, La Compagnie de Jésus, no. 63, p. 235.
76. Thwaites, Jesuit Relations, XVI, 233.
77. Thwaites, Jesuit Relations, XVII, 13.
78. Thwaites, Jesuit Relations, XXXIX, 175. This letter is the basis of the account given by Bressani in his "Brief Relation" and also of the Relation of 1647, XXI, 17.
79. Martin-Shea, Father Isaac Jogues, S. J., p. 114–5.
80. Ibid., Idem, p. 124.
81. Ibid., Idem, p. 127.
82. Ibid. Idem, p. 133–4.
83. Ibid., Idem, p. 135–6.
84. Thwaites, Jesuit Relations, XXV, p. 288.
85. Ibid., Idem, XXXVIII, p. 207.
86. Ibid., Idem, XXXI, p. 17.
87. Ibid., Idem, XXVII, p. 247.
88. Shea, p. 186.

Ref.
No.

89. Thwaites, Jesuit Relations, XXXI, 113.
90. Ibid., Idem, XXIII, 251.
91. Ibid., Idem, XXV, 25.
92. Ibid., Idem, XXVI, 265.
93. Ibid., Idem, XXXIV, 87.
94. Ibid., Idem, XXXIV, 139.
95. Ibid., Idem, XXXV, 107, 163.
96. Ibid., Idem, XL, 255.
97. Ibid., Idem, XXXV, 151.
98. Ibid., Idem, XXV, 31-33.
99 Apocalypse, v, 9.
100. The Pilgrim of Our Lady of Martyrs (1910), XXVI, 134-141.
101. Thwaites, Jesuit Relations, L, 123; LVI, 103.
102. Ibid., Idem, LII, 141.
103. Ibid., Idem, XXXIV, 227.
104. Ibid., Idem, LX, 181.

BIBLIOGRAPHY

Bancroft, George: History of the United States (Boston, 1850).

Bracq, Jean Charlemagne: The Evolution of French Canada (New York, 1924).

Brodhead, John Romeyn: History of the State of New York (New York, 1853–71).

Brucker, Joseph, S. J.: La Compagnie de Jésus (Paris, 1919).

Buteux, Jacques: The Capture of Father Jogues, tr. in The Pilgrim of Our Lady of Martyrs (January-December, 1896).

Campbell, Thomas J., S. J.: The Jesuits, 1534–1921 (New York, 1921).

Campbell, Thomas J., S. J.: Pioneer Priests of North America, 1642–1710 (New York, 1908).

Catholic Encyclopedia (16 vols., New York, 1913).

Charlevoix, François-Xavier: Histoire et description générale de la Nouvelle France (Paris, 1744), tr. Shea (New York, 1866–72).

Ferland, Jean-Baptiste-Antoine: Histoire du Canada (Quebec, 1884).

Finley, John: The French in the Heart of America (New York, 1918).

Fouqueray, Henri, S. J.: Histoire de la Compagnie de Jésus en France, vols. II–III (Paris, 1913–22).

Garneau, François-Xavier: Histoire du Canada (Paris, 1920).

Goyau, Georges: Histoire religieuse de la nation française (Paris, 1922).

Goyau, Georges: Les origines religieuses du Canada (Paris, 1924).

Hanotaux, Gabriel: Histoire de la nation française (15 vols., Paris, 1920–24).

Jones, Arthur Edward, S. J.: Old Huronia; in Fraser, Ontario Archives (Toronto, 1909).

Lafitau, Joseph–François: Mœurs des Sauvages Americains (Paris, 1724).

Le Clercq, Christian: Premier Établissement de la Foi dans la Nouvelle France (Paris, 1691, tr. Shea (New York, 1881).

Martin, Felix, S. J.: Hurons et Iroquois: Le P. Jean de Brébeuf (Paris, 1877).

Martin, Felix, S. J.: R. P. Isaac Jogues (Paris, 1877), tr. Shea, The Life of Fr. Isaac Jogues (New York, 1885).

O'Callaghan, E. B.: Documentary History of the State of New York (Albany, 1849–51).

Parkman, Francis: The Jesuits in North America in the Seventeenth Century (Boston, 1868).

THE JESUIT MARTYRS

Pilgrim of Our Lady of Martyrs (1886 to date).

Richard, Edouard: Acadia, ed. Henri D'Arles (3 vols., Quebec, 1898–1903.

Rochemonteix, Camille de, S. J.: Les Jésuites et la Nouvelle France (Paris, 1896). tr. Pilgrim of Our Lady of Martyrs, 1898–1903.

Sagard, Thédat–Gabriel: Le grand Voyage du Pays des Hurons (Paris, 1865).

Sagard, Théodat-Gabriel: Histoire du Canada (Paris, 1686).

INDEX

INDEX

INDEX

Garnier, Charles, 15, 107; wounded, 213; death, 214; burial, 215.
Goupil, René, 16 sq.; captured by Iroquois, 156; torture, 158, 163 sq.; refuses to escape, 162; death, 171; burial, 172 sqq.
Grammar, of Huron language, 116.
Guercheville, Madame de, 31 sqq.
Hebert, family, 76 sq.
Hell, appeal to Indians, 80.
Henry IV, King of France, 28, 31.
Hubou, Guillaume, 77.
Huguenots, 7, 28 sq., 41 sq., 63 sq.
Huronia, 152.
Huron language, studied by missionaries, 94, 117; Potier's books, 6.
Hurons, 54 sqq., 149; and Franciscans, 39; timidity, 95; hostility to Jesuits, 121, 124; conversions, 193 sqq.; and Iroquois, 96, 156, 158 sqq., 209 sqq.; exterminated, 222.
Ihonatiria, 84; life at, 112.
Imbert, Simon, 34.
Immaculate Virgin, mission dedicated to, 90.
Indian language, difficulties of translation, 148.
Insects, 94.
Invocation, of Jesuit martyrs, 226 sq.
Iroquois, 152 sqq.; peace conference, 188 sqq.; hostility to Hurons, 96, 197; cruelty to women, 211 sqq.
Jamet, Denis, 39, 41.
Jansen, Jacob, 175.
Jeanne, Algonquin, 164.
Jesuit Relations, 68 sqq.
Jesuits, 17; colleges in France, 1600, 4 sqq.; missions, 9; martyrs in Japan, Poland, England, 10; education, 18; novitiate, 18 sqq.; obedience, 138.
Jogues, Isaac, 13; at Quebec, 1636, 33; letters to his mother, 107; journey to Ihonatiria, 106 sq.; dream, 121; at Quebec, 1642, 152; captured by Iroquois, 153; account of captivity, 154 sqq.; torture, 158 sqq.; as slave of Mohawks, 175 sqq.; escape, 184; return to France, 186; return to Canada, 187; ambassador to Iroquois, 188 sq.; death, 190; memorials, 229.
Kerkt, David, and brothers, 61, 63 sq.
Kieft, William, 185.
Labatie, Jean, 175.
Lalande, Jean de, 17; death, 190.
Lalemant, Charles, 22, 43; "Relations," 69.
Lalemant, Gabriel, 16, 137; martyrdom, 201 sqq.
Lalemant, Jerome, 121, 189.
Lay companions of missionaries, 16, 139, 156, 158.

INDEX

INDEX

INDEX